How To ...
in the
Middle

Management Cadre

Without
Blood Pressure, Heart Attack & Ulcers

Dr P. V. Pathak

BUSINESS PUBLICATIONS INC

Dedicated to my late mother, Smt. Shalini Pathak, whose reading habit I inherit.

To all my maternal uncles

Shri B.S.Deshpande alias Anna Mama
Shri A.S. Deshpande alias Bal Mama
Shri V.S Deshpande alias Viju Mama
and Shri S.S Deshpande alias Kaka Mama
whom I owe my emotional integration .

© Dr P V Pathak, 1998
ISBN 81-86982-28-0

Cover design and illustrations by Puneet Bareja
Printed by Black Dots, Mumbai

Published by

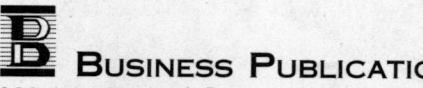

BUSINESS PUBLICATIONS INC
229 / A Second floor
Krantiveer Rajguru Marg
Girgaon Mumbai 400 004

CONTENTS

This book today keeps the health hazards away.

THE PURPOSE

*Today, when survival with a healthy
body is a boon, it is attitude that matters.
Mould yourself to be free from tension
and ailments arising from that tension.*

The three health hazards, **Blood Pressure, Heart Attack** and **Ulcers** in the stomach, are classified by modern medicine as ailments of old age. As age slowly asserts mastery over the body mechanism, the individual may yield to any of these three ailments. However, it is observed that many managers and junior executives in good firms often fall prey to these health hazards at an early age. So much so, that these ailments have come to be regarded as occupational health hazards. One often becomes prone to these ailments from excessive anxiety, excitement, frustration and prolonged hard work without any fruitful conclusion coming within sight. These are the typical circumstances in which modern executives have to work over long years, and hence they are found to be more susceptible to these ailments. In the pages that follow, the reader will find tips for middle management personnel, to help them avoid these three ailments as far as possible.

The title of this book may remind you of having seen a similar title elsewhere. Yes! It comes from the Indian management wizard, R.K.Rustomji, who has specified a path leading to the top the without succumbing to these three health hazards (*How to go to the top without having ulcer, heart attack and blood pressure*).

I am not sure whether the material you are about to read will pave the way for the middle management cadre person to reach the top, but it will surely help him to hold back three health hazards which may be subduing his health surreptitiously. But to avoid having people pointing a finger at me for the heinous crime of plagiarisation, I acknowledge right here the debt to two of my *Gurus*, R.K. Rustomji and Shri Sharu Ranganekar, neither of whom I have had the privilege of meeting. Their profound influence will be felt by the reader throughout the text. Like Ekalavya, from the *Mahabharata*, I call them my *Gurus* and go ahead.

Here is the first and foremost lesson for those for whom this text is to serve the solemn purpose of guidance and advice: *Do not try to take undue credit for the things which are widely known.* If you do, you end up with many fingers being pointed at you.

Here we are going to deal with the problems faced every now and then by people of the MIDDLE MANAGEMENT CADRE, hereafter referred to as the MMC, especially in concerns and production plants which manufacture items for marketing. They are the shopfloor people, often in supervisory or junior executive posts. We suggest to them certain remedial attitudes (not measures), to keep away these life-destroying parasites forever, unless, of course, one's genes are designed to acquire them. And even if that be so, let time take care of them, rather than you expediting their takeover on the way to the top. Many of the tips and advice given herein may be found useful by members of the MMC from other sections of industry as well. But no generalizations or universal principles are suggested. The author has no sermon to offer. He only attempts to share his experience with the younger generation members of the MMC who own are now striving to achieve the goal at some cost. Having experienced both the anxiety and excitement, he feels he has something to share with the younger generation of the MMC, to which he earlier belonged.

This book will, of course, be read by those who have crossed the MMC barrier and are in positions where they have to deal with MMC juniors. For them, it may  serve the purpose of reminiscing on the bad old days when they too slogged, struggled and some times slothed under bosses whom they could not properly understand. It is also to remind them of the role of daughter-in-law that they had to play once. And now, in their present commanding position, **not** to play the role of harsh and inconsiderate mother-in-law, as sometimes happens in traditional Indian family settings. This reminder can perhaps help them to view their juniors with an enlightened and experienced outlook.

The author is reminded of a parable associated with the great savant and saint of the last century, Shri Ramakrishna Paramhansa.

Once a lady took her child to Shri Ramakrishna, complaining that the child often ate a lot of jaggery. She requested him to admonish the child and said only his powerful words would serve the purpose. Shri Ramakrishna asked her to come back after a week. When the lady again visited the great man along with her child, he, in his genial manner, told the child not to indulge in excessive jaggery eating. Seeing the casual way Shri Ramakrishna was talking to the child, the lady got upset. She told Shri Ramakrishna that just to tell the child not to eat too much jaggery she need not have come a second time. He could as well have told the child this during the last visit. Shri Ramakrishna smiled and told her that he did not believe in preaching without practising. For a week he too, had not eaten jaggery and had found that it was hard to totally abstain from eating sweets. But having done it, he was now in a position to understand the child's mind and was talking to him accordingly.

Similarly, it is difficult for highflyers from many prestigious management institutions, fellows who directly jumped onto the management band-wagon at the higher berths and who suffer from the mother-in-law syndrome from the beginning, to know and appreciate the pangs of their slogging juniors. This book, which is the collective experience of a few MMC fellows, can help these highflyers to understand the mind of their juniors, change their ways if they be harsh and so reduce the burden on them. However, the author is aware of his limitations. This world is vast and changing so fast. With limited experience, one should not commit the folly of universalizing one's conclusions. That shuts the doors on further information inputs. In today's world, there is an information explosion and shutting oneself off to new inputs can only prove detrimental to one's understanding of issues.

While reading the text, you are requested to follow certain mental disciplines. You should carefully note the quotes and unquotes, commas and brackets; which are intentionally used to convey something beyond what mere words can convey. One should not jump over to the next sentence unless one is clear about the previous one.

One can expect remedial measures to be suggested in this book, implying that once these measures are implemented, one can look forward to the solution of the problem. However, this is not always the case. Indian methods of management are a wee bit different. Very often, Indian management is interested in shutting out the problem, leaving it to be faced by the MMC. Under these circumstances, it is your attitude that will take care of your welfare. Therefore, the author has given ways and means of moulding one's attitude rather than listing the remedial measures.

Many case studies presented here are first-hand experiences. However, the rest have been gathered through friends and co-workers in the profession and from informal interviews, usually over breakfast or a cup of tea. One may find that some of these tally completely with the reader's own experiences. Although one cannot have access to everybody's life

Watering hole discussions about the boss.

experiences, it does serve to confirm that things are no better elsewhere. It is also a matter of solace and has a soothing effect, like daughters-in-law exchanging notes over the behavioural patterns of their mother-in-law. However, a word of caution here, too much of solace seeking is also not good. It will keep you back in your daughter-in-law syndrome. So better come out. The remedial attitudes suggested here are for getting rid of this daughter-in-law syndrome. There is an extreme example worth quoting here.

A CASE STUDY

In a public limited company, a group of MMCs had established a very good relationship amongst themselves and with their immediate boss. This was brought about by a MMC fellow who used to take the initiative in organising dinner parties periodically. During these parties the boss and the MMCs would talk freely and decide their course of action till the next meet. Especially on the labour front, they would talk about catching a labour leader indulging in out-of-the-routine activities. Once it so happened that the boss could not attend the party. At the party, all the MMCs discussed the failures of the boss and nothing else. For once it was alright. But when it happened again, it was like daughters-in-law of the village meeting at the water hole and discussing only the bad points of their respective mothers-in-law. The initiative-taking MMC man realised the intensity of the daughter-in-law syndrome in his colleagues and left in a huff.

There is a large number of organised sector employees in our country, typically in the Governmental sector, the public sector or in large companies, who do not discuss anything in their leisure time but their bosses's failures or their own increments, P.F, bonus and any demands they may have. This is what the author calls the daughter-in-law syndrome, resulting from the perpetual feeling of persecution at the hands of the people in power. So! Get rid of it. There are many good things happening around. Get to know them. Indulge in them and that can surely help to keep the deadly threesome away.

IDENTIFY YOURSELF

*Knowing oneself is the greatest
achievement. Know thyself and you
know the boss. Do not hesitate in
identifying your category. It can help you
to outline your lifestyle on the shopfloor.*

Since man started taking the help of his fellow human beings by paying a price for the help, there have been conflicting versions of any incident. The versions are always coloured by one's attitude and to which group one belongs. Under these conditions it is better to identify oneself. The ancient *rishis* wisely proclaimed, '*Jnattva pindam, jnatam brahmandam*', 'Know thyself and you will know the Universe'. This maxim holds true not only in spiritual life but in the most mundane matters, in dealings with your own mind, on the shopfloor and with the boss.

Know that you belong to the MIDDLE MANAGEMENT CADRE, i.e. you do not belong to the class of manual workers or labourers. It implies that you do not have the privilege of forming a union and taking your legitimate (or illegitimate) grievances to a committee or a registered union. Then, as a union member, your personal involvement in solving your problems or removing the cause of grievance, is minimized. Somebody else, the union leader speaks to the management on your behalf, even commits harakiri for you but you are saved. This door being closed, your acceptance into the class of organized workers comes to nought.

You are neither acceptable in the class of 'management', which consists basically of the ruling elite (or clique?). This class can do and undo the fate of those below their cadre. While a union membership can help its members in the case of promotions, leaves or adverse confidentials being expunged, in your case, your fate is sealed. It is being akin to the erstwhile *Kshatriya* warrior, who having lost one battle, irrespective of whether he had won many earlier ones, was branded a loser. He had to either win or die. Rajput kings of the medieval period typify this attitude. There was no successful retreat for these Rajput kings, a tactic that British generals successfully adopted. To the Rajputs, once lost was lost forever. Then the chances are for those who do not dare to commit any act and are therefore free from the blemish of being losers. Their CRs (confidential reports) remain blemish-free.

One is reminded here of the French hero, Napoleon Bonaparte I. While selecting colonels for his army, he selected a man with a winning record. And you know where the poor chap had to end up— at St. Helena, under the hawkish eyes of the British command. The Napoleonic traits of Indian management will be dealt with later in the book. Here we are concerned with your class identification. You belong to the *Kshatriya* class, the warriors, whose solemn duty was to protect society. In today's society, it is to keep the wheels of production running. The *Kshatriya* was expected to hazard death in order to gain heavenly luxuries as his sacred reward. While ancient heros like Arjuna and Bhima, could enjoy these luxuries here on earth, in the post-*Mahabharata* war years, the same cannot be written in your fate. There are far too many others to share these rewards with you. Look at the population growth, especially in the management cadre. They eat away the bulk of your share in running the show.

A better analogy from the epic story can be offered, featuring the hero Bhima and the middle son. It is a story of a *Brahmin* boy whose family was held captive by the demon Ghatotkacha. The demon was searching for a human being to be offered to his mother for breakfast. While the father could not spare the eldest son who was about to take over the father's earning profession, the youngest was dear to the mother. Thus, the middle son was the only one who could be dispensed with. When it came to really handing over the middle son, Bhima, accidentally appeared on the scene just as the demon called out for the middle son to come out and be the collective family offering. The story ends with the reunion of Bhima with Ghatokacha's mother, who was his forgotten but once enamoured lady. He also acted as godfather to the middle son of the captive family. This comedy may not take place in your case.

The Modern Industrial Caste Structure

In the present organizational structure of Indian industry, the top managerial cadre is like the eldest son of the Brahmin. For whatever reasons, best known to the top people, the managerial cadre is normally well looked after with various perks and perquisites. You can even gauge this from the numerous ads in newspapers for managerial staff, which appear with bold letters and display, while those for the MMC appear in the classified columns with super concessional rate offers from the newspapers. Discrimination starts right here.

 The labourers-workers also receive paternalistic treatment from their organised unions. The union leaders are out to protect the interests of their fellow union members. So the onus of carrying out assigned duties falls on your shoulders and for failure in carrying out these duties, the MMC is the scapegoat ready to be sacrificed.

A more apt but rather sardonic analogy to your position can be given. It is that of an owl. This creature is traditionally classified neither as animal and thus trot about on their legs, nor it is given the status of birds, who do not look back to earthly problems. The MMC fellow is also a sure omen for both the classes they deal with. The analogy of an OWL can be further illustrated.

You are an ominous sight on weekends for the boss-cum-manager, who is in a holiday mood and arranging the weekend outing as you enter his cabin with an oblong face. Looking at you he knows at once. Surely you are bringing him a problem from the shop-floor. Is it a labour problem? In that case one does not expect anything other than a bit of a sermon, a firing and some advice about interpersonal relations. He declares that the problem has arisen because of lack of understanding of your work, lack of rapport with workers, or you cannot motivate them and so on. When you see that your boss is in no mood to look into the immediate problems, you withdraw. There are many reasons for not presenting these to him. For instance, even if you have caught a notorious chap red-handed, under these circumstances it is better to rely on the natural gift of two ears to keep away the health hazards. Remember that nature has bestowed human beings with a pair of ears, that too, in a straight line. There is very little distance in-between the two. So never let that sermon or whatever, enter your brain. Always keep one ear (a natural option) open for letting it straight out. It helps to keep your cool. Understand that it is he your boss, who can do or undo the future and has the power to motivate the workers. It is not your lot. The means of motivation are beyond your reach. Think that words are nothing but ordered vibrations. Let them not pierce your skin. If it is that soft, harden it a bit. It helps.

About being an ominous sign, you are certainly one for a (it is always 'a') worker waiting outside the certainly manager's cabin. For you can catch only 'a' worker. After meeting with the boss, you came out with a grim face, overflowing with frustration. You are an ominous sign for a chap you have caught, a poor chap for the time being (till he does not fall back on union support). You have caught him red-handed. You are about to give expression to your accumulated rage and feelings suppressed over a long period. You feel this is the opportunity to fire him. It is time to show him who you are. You also want to bring to the notice of the management the efforts you have made to catch this notorious character. Mind you, do not explode! You have not received proper response from your boss. So, stop for a while, count 100 and cool down. Be satisfied with the fact that you have, for once, had the upper hand in dealing with the chap. He will think twice before he comes to talk to you next time. Your becoming an omnious sign for him is enough for the present.

Is it then that you are a nonentity? No! Don't be nervous. It is not that you do not matter, or that you do not do anything. You are the one who is directly concerned with the proceedings (and not the production only) on the shopfloor. As a responsible person, you sign on the daily log sheet and know the production line intimately. You are paid for it. As long as the payment part remains intact, you are not to worry about anything. Occasionally you can do a favour to your juniors or workers and be happy by acting the good Samaritan. You can exercise whatever little power you have for the well meaning workers if not for them all. You can create your own group of reliable workers. This always helps to a certain extent. But a caution here. Do not let this group of reliables or faithfuls grow too large. It is harmful.

 The very fact that you had to enter the MMC implies that you posses something more than those who belong to the workers' category. You certainly lack something that would have enabled you to grace the upper echelons of management. It is like having been born into a particular *jati*, it takes immense effort and time to cross the *jati* barrier. From ancient times, when the population too was much less, there is one name worth mentioning, i.e. the sage *Vishvamitra*. He attained *Brahmin*hood in spite of being born a *Kshatriya*. This possibility of jumping the caste barrier has improved in modern times, especially in the industrial sector. There might even be persons around you, who have crossed the MMC and acquired the top managerial status. You can look to them for inspiration but not guidance; in the latter case you are sure to be misled. Here comes another consideration to complicate the picture. Here you have to exercise your own discretion. To which of the following types of MMCs do you belong? Assess yourself.

A Few Words About Categorization

In the literature available, you will come across the various types of categories, classes and types of MMCs, bosses, industrial undertakings and so on. In this book, you will normally come across only three types, the fourth being exceptional. Why only three categories? Because we are not interested in conducting hair-splitting research, say for the purpose of submitting a Ph.D. thesis in industrial psychology.

If you look at various natural phenomena that are quantified in terms of mathematical equations, you come across only three types: Zero, first and second order equations. It is very rare that one comes across any phenomenon needing a third or higher order of expression. Even the mass energy equivalence equation proposed by the great physicist Albert Einstein, is no more complex than the second order. It can be observed that usually threesome classifications meet the requirements of day-to-day understanding of mundane occurrences in our lives. Here I draw support from the all-time great management wizard, Lord Krishna. He ably managed to pull his chums out of a gambling disaster. He too, has classified all human beings into three categories only : *sattvik, rajas,* and *tamas.* This classification has not yet been successfully challenged by any of the great and talented commentators starting with Adi Shankara to Lokmanya Tilak, who have debated on the message Lord Krishna had to convey. Possibly the Lord too, had to follow the natural phenomena governed by the maximum second order equation; or perhaps he could not disown (like your boss?) his own divine creation. But remember that he has categorically stated during his discourse, that he does not belong to any of these three classes. The same thing applies to many others who are like him, i.e. the exceptional cases. So, anytime you come across something exceptional, remember it is a divine occurance.

CATEGORIES OF MMC FELLOWS

From the point of view of the management (that, of course, is what matters,) the people of the MMC fall into three categories :

CATEGORY A - Genial, gentle, sincere, obedient, reliable, motivated and so on. It is not so bad, in fact , rather a good assessment.

CATEGORY B - Cool, steadfast, a single-track mind, SUITED FOR BEING MMC ONLY.

CATEGORY C - Aggressive, impolite, ill-motivated, unreliable, succumbing to the machinations of the other workers.

All these code words for categories A, B and C, are coined to make it clear which category, in the eyes of the management, one belongs to. All three types from the MMC can aspire to rise to the top but one can never be sure as to when and why. None can guarantee that it will be only the people of category A or at the most category B, who will rise. Not so. The fellows from category C too can rise. Another important aspect to note here is that your category in the eyes of the management depends mostly on your boss, to whom you have to report every now and then. To be clear, management looks at you through the eyes of your boss. And so your category depends mostly on his assessment.

Categories of MMC Fellows
A : Genial   B : Cool   C : Aggressive

It can change with a change of boss and his perception of your ability. There can be many reasons for your belonging to a particular category. Everything in this world is transient, as the Lord Buddha proclaimed—*sabbam anicham*. For the time being, in the given set-up, all that you have to know about yourself is which category you belong to. Accordingly you can chart your strategy to keep the health hazards away.

Do not ever try to put yourself in the shoes of exceptional cases. You dare not follow their path. There are many constraints which these exceptional fellows have easily overcome to jump over the MMC barrier. You will not.

A CASE STUDY

This is the case of an engineer with a sober background (The FIRST CONSTRAINT). Within a month or two of joining his company, the company received a big export order (The SECOND CONSTRAINT). Being newly appointed and therefore highly motivated to make a mark, he took up the challenge (The THIRD CONSTRAINT). He was a person with a sports background, i.e. possessing team spirit (The FOURTH CONSTRAINT). He offered due credit to all those who mattered during the production schedule. He achieved the target within a permissible delay period. His enthusiasm was noted by the MD who used to be on regular rounds during this period (The FIFTH CONSTRAINT).

After the consignment was despatched, for some unavoidable reasons, he was required to visit the MD's residence on quite a few occasions. He was good looking, smart and well mannered. The MD's marriageable daughter took a fancy to him (the SIXTH and the most unusual CONSTRAINT) and he was soon married to her. In no time he was sitting next to the MD's chair. The sixth constraint is a one-in-a-million chance, and therefore it is to be classified in the exceptional category. The circumstances which could have been considered major constraints normally, proved advantageous in this case.

CATEGORIES CHARACTER MAPS

Mapping is a vital function in modern-day management. All types of production and core functions are being mapped. Here is an attempt to map your mindscape according to the category to which you belong. It is subject to corrections if pointed out. This is a general categorization of behaviour. The finer points should be noted by yourself from your own experiences.

CATEGORY A

Do you consider yourself to belong to category A? If so, you have a survival oriented nature. You have learnt life's lesson that only the management can do or undo your future. It is certainly a sign of maturity. Therefore, you defend each and every step taken by the management. You sincerely consider it to be the correct step and given a chance, you will follow in the same footsteps.

You most earnestly feel that the management should be aware of everything that goes on within the precincts of the establishment. In a way the management, too, considers it to be necessary. So you are always eager to convey the news of whatever little happens (mostly wrong) in the plant. By doing this, you are establishing that you are truly faithful to your company. This attitude is encouraged by the top management in most cases. But then you have lost your peace. While your attitude becomes servile towards the top, your esteem in the eyes of other colleagues of your own rank and below and also the workers, goes down. It even reaches a stage when you will be treated contemptuously by them.

There is also a bit of danger in becoming over enthusiastic in the delicate matter of these upward communications. Somebody may deliberately introduce a missing but actually erroneous link which may be exposed at an opportune time. Then you become a laughing stock. Here again you are likely to lose your cool. So be careful. Assess the information before passing it upwards.

For obvious reasons, you are labelled as an informer. To use an Indian colloquial term, you have become 'management ka chamcha'. During crises like strikes, lockouts, or dharanas, you become an easy target for denigration. It is often the people of category 'A' who have suffered greatly for the sake of the management and sometimes even laid down their own lives. You cannot help whatever happens to you under these circumstances.

*Never enter into arguments
with armed opponents.*

What remedial attitude should you develop? Understand yourself. You cannot help what you are. Remember an old and ever-true adage, 'Might (SUBSTITUTE MANAGEMENT) is Right'. Maturity in your attitude keeps away the thoughts that may prick your conscience. Let it not exist, is the first dictum for you. Secondly, feelings of esteem and so on are only ephemeral emotions. So long as you are in the good books of the management, you can always boast about being so outside your factory premises, i.e. with the neighbours, relatives, especially the in-laws. During periods of tension; during personnel problems, you may be booed, awkwardly treated by workers, vehemently argued with by your juniors. Understand it as part of the game.

On such occasions, argue out the issue with the fellow workers who tend to be argumentative. They are harmless. But never enter into an argument with those who wield weapons such as knives and so on. You know who they are.

After the argument you have given vent to your feelings. This type of relief is necessary even from a health point of view. Having done so, you have achieved reduction in your acidity. It keeps ulcers away. In the case of altercations, if you have not let these last for more than SEVEN MINUTES, you have achieved relief from blood pressure, which otherwise will remain smouldering within you to flare up sometime later. Only for those who already have heart trouble, here is a little hint. Argue, but without aggression and without raising your voice. During an argument, if the other guy gets out of control, remind him of your heart trouble. Ask him to take it on humanitarian grounds. Tell him that these types of flare ups only lead to heart trouble. You will find him suddenly cooling down. It will help you both to come back to the right track.

The occasional outburst of pent-up emotions, of course in favour of your management, is always helpful for you. It raises your esteem in the eyes of the management.

CATEGORY B

People belonging to category B are men of steadfast nature and cool in their approach. Normally they mind their job and treat it as their solemn duty. They are fully aware of what they are being paid for. They sincerely believe that if one discharges one's duty, doing one's best, one can aspire to rise to a higher position. This possibly makes them look like people with a single-track mind. But the world not being so straight-forward, somebody always changes his track (wrong track for you), bypassing you to jump ahead.

Do you belong to category B? If so, you take an interest in your job to the extent that it comes to the notice of those who matter. This is advantageous for your juniors, especially on the shopfloor, where technical problems crop up every now and then. Juniors and workers can rely on you for the solution to these problems. Your depth of knowledge, your sincerity, hard work and so on, earn you extra prestige. This is a matter of great satisfaction. Try not to indulge in any petty politics going around. Keep aloof. It reduces resistance to your authority on the shopfloor. However, this sometimes results in being considered as demotivation by some of those who assess you for promotion. They are the ones who consider people of category A as being more reliable. You cannot help these people assessing you. At this juncture they may consider you better suited for shopfloor jobs only. You may get an additional increment at the year end but not promotion.

Because of your nature, you are not a good personnel relations man unless you possess it as an inborn quality or on realizing it, acquire extra initiative in this regard. Your technical capabilities or other achievements either reach in a toned down manner to where it matters, or do not reach at all. Without your initiative in cultivating good relations with your boss, or a sympathizer in the top echelons of the company, nobody can further your cause.

There are also certain strong points in your personality. Because of your indulgence in work, you possess a higher sustaining power in mundane matters like promotions, increments and so on. Being confident of your own ability and also having perseverance in-built into your personality, it takes a little longer for these three health hazards to come to grips with you.

What happens if some junior supersedes you or you are deprived of your due credit or share in a particular achievement, from your point of view, of course? Your reaction is that of utter frustration. Once you allow this feeling to build up within yourself, in one short week you will become a completely changed personality.

This week normally begins from a day on which either a much more junior person or a less competent person comes in as your boss and he starts dictating terms. Either you start searching for another job, if you are ready to face the challenge of re-establishing your position in a new concern and soon move out, or for some personal reasons like your wife having permanent employment in the same place or the education of the children or some other sort of problem, you are forced to remain in the same concern. It brings about a sea change in your personality. You start pooh-poohing the promoted chap in the presence of your juniors who know him too. Sometimes you deliberately withhold important details which otherwise you would have easily revealed. Your frustation finds expression in your normal talk. If you are a person who takes shopfloor problems home, your family starts encountering problems too. Your first reaction in that case will be to remind your family members, especially your growing up children, how much you have toiled for them.

In case you are superseded by a person who is more capable, you become even more frustrated. In the case where he does not deserve to be your superior, you could at least give verbal expression to your feelings and relieve your tension. But in this case, where a capable person supersedes you, you can start gathering raw materials that attract the hazardous threesome. If this continues for a little longer, your sick leave record lengthens. You remain a likable personality no more.

Herein comes the need for attitudinal change in your outlook. The first thing you should understand is that only sincerity or shopfloor technical expertise (whatever you label it yourself) is enough to bring you laurels but no promotions. It is part of professional self realization and a sign of maturity. The very fact that somebody has superseded you results in delaying your promotion. Take it for granted that your chances to rise up to the higher position are further delayed, at least till that person moves higher up and you mend fences with him. Considering that the fellow superseding you, is himself new to this position for a time. He too needs peace. Understanding his expectations will help you to mend fences with him.

How to tackle this situation? Here are some hints. Once you have accepted in your heart of hearts this delay, it helps you to soothe yourself. The expressions of frustration and so on get toned down. You do not become a less likable person to your colleagues. Keep your esteem intact. Take the situation gracefully and grace never leaves you.

However, the mind is a very complex thing. It is really very difficult not to get frustrated. A little introspection can help you to understand the frustration gripping you. Under these conditions there is a unique solution worth trying.

Take your most near and dear one, perhaps your wife, into your confidence. Talk to her in private about your frustration and you can be sure of sincere and heartfelt sympathy. If you have not opened your mind earlier, she too will feel satisfied and be emotionally closer and  more loving. You have to take the next most important step. Go on a long trip. Do not plan your outing to Kulu Manali or Shimla. There, a man of technical bent like you, may find only monotonous greenery. You may not enjoy it for more than 2-3 days. It is your nature. Also, do not take a guided tour organised by a travel agency to the so-called places of tourist interest. Chalk out a tour programme to some unusual places anywhere in the country. During this trip, try to cover as many places as possible. Try to prepare your background knowledge about these places. There is no dearth of such lesser-known but exotic places. Say you are going to south India, try to understand temple structuring. Try to discover who built the temple and when. Think of drawing say PERT/CPM diagrams for the temple construction as if you have been entrusted with the task. If you intend to visit the eastern states, try to study the cultural aspects of the tribes. Their social norms are different. There can be many interesting things to study. Turn the trip into your second honeymoon. It may cost you a bit more but the cost is worth paying. Forget the shopfloor for these days. Enjoy the trip thoroughly.

 When you come back, you are a rejuvenated personality. On the home front, which may matter more hence after, your valuation has been elevated. Possibly you have treated it so far as of secondary importance. After a pretty long time you may finally have done justice to your family committments. So the family reciprocate with warmth. You have a feeling of being desired.

To your colleagues and workers around you, you remain the same graceful person. And now that you can add a few interesting tidbits and anecdotes from your tour, you become a more likable person as well. This is no mean achievement. You act normal, just as you used to be. This will not escape the eyes of the management.

There is another aspect that the management cannot ignore, your prolonged absence from the shopfloor will have been certainly felt by them. Your rejoining may be welcomed by the boss, who, realising your potential, can strongly recommend your case the next time.

A CASE STUDY

After the second world war, the English voter routed the Churchill government. Winston Churchill was, in fact, the person who brought victory to the nation.

Although he himself won the parliamentary seat, his party lost. He had to face a similar situation after the total rout of his party. He started having similar bouts of frustration. His wife was a very wise lady (a fortunate circumstance). She packed bags for both of them and took him on a long tour to the U.S.A. There, the great man was given a hero's welcome. His ego was satisfied. He came back rejuvenated from the tour and continued to grace the opposition benches in parliament. He also accomplished the mammoth task of writing six volumes of World War II memoirs. He again fought the election and became Prime Minister. But for the wise decision of Mrs Churchill, Sir Winston Churchill a chain smoker, would have been a ready victim to any of these three health hazards.

Category C

If you belong to this category, you have a very volatile nature. No one can bottle you. Your nature itself enthuses you to go on extending your horizons. You become a quicksilver personality. In the days of leftist movements, you could not avoid becoming aware of class struggle, capitalist hegemony, bourgeoisie mentality and so on. Today, leftist movements and unionism have taken a back seat. Even the labour class behaves like the bourgeoise and unions are not interested in touting the harangue of class struggle. The Marxist idol, Jyoti Basu, openly invites the

Multinationals for capital investment in West Bengal and none cries hoarse when the labour laws are amended in favor of capitalists and accountability. But these days the issues are different. Your heart can continue to bleed for the downtrodden labourers and deprived sections of society, until by virtue of your position, you realise the negative traits also present in them. You are aware of the scope of human rights, the pollution potential of your company and the suffering it inflicts on the workers and the surroundings. You are truly sympathetic towards contract labourers who continue to do the hard work. You are considerate of the class below and naturally upright before the higher ups. Because of your 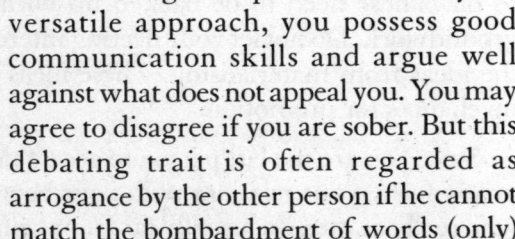 versatile approach, you possess good communication skills and argue well against what does not appeal you. You may agree to disagree if you are sober. But this debating trait is often regarded as arrogance by the other person if he cannot match the bombardment of words (only) from you. It may possibly be regarded as veiled threats. If the other person has an authoritative nature and also possesses authority to match, he can just cut you short during discussions.

Because of your nature, you are taken as a self-willed person (which you may not be) and difficult to deal with (a fact). Your leaning towards the labourers and espousing their cause may create suspicion in the minds of the management. And accordingly, you may get treatment meted out as to a secondary citizen. As you are voluble person, conversely you get less attention, thereby fewer opportunities to open your mouth and therefore, less of a hearing from those on the top. This also results in your lagging behind on the ladder to the top position.

On technical matters, you may prove to be superior to your colleagues. But check whether your volatile nature prevents you from taking a deep interest in technical matters. Or does your interest in technical matters. Or does your interest in anything also vapourises quickly? This is a sign of lack of perseverance and capacity to follow up. You may come out with some brilliant ideas in improving the process, efficiency and so on. These need to be backed up with adequate groundwork. Do not let your fleeting interest prevent the ideas from materialising. These ideas may open up chances for promotion.

Since you are the last person to accept domination in any form, your relations with your boss and those who really matter, are usually far from being normal. You are an outspoken person and carry the aura of being a militant personality. Your boss and those above you are certainly aware of your potential and as human beings propelled by the instinct for self-survival, they may try to nip your enthusiasm in the bud.

For you, all those around you are equal while in your heart of hearts you also feel yourself to be the first among equals. Depending on the sobriety of your nature and other personality traits, you may indulge in schemes for toppling or exposing your boss. In small family concerns this is bit difficult but in the corporate or public sector, you are likely to become a tool in the hands of some top men scheming against each other. Guard against this danger.

People of your type cannot overcome mental tensions. They are prone to attacks of the threesome. Before you have understood yourself you have had it. In a way you are a lucky man. You possess the mental capability of looking at yourself from a third person's point-of-view. Once you have understood the game being played at various levels, you can easily overcome the tensions arising out of the situation. You can soon learn the art of keeping tensions and worries at a distance. To others you may be the person who explodes on little provocation. But you know you are enjoying it. In fact, you may create a tense situation for your boss. No amount of pressure applied on you serves to straighten you out. Your boss may pass sleepless nights on your account. Even in the wake of being thrown out, you make sure that a few more heads roll along with yours

You cannot aspire to rise in any one organisation because of your nature. Hence you are prone to changing situations more frequently than others. And then age takes its toll. Over the years, your aging body refuses to cooperate with your volatile spirit. You mellow down and have a chance  of becoming somebody in one organisation. By then you have learnt to be a good administrator who can control the tug-of-war going on between the management and the workers.

A CASE STUDY

This instance is taken from the textile industry where people shift over from one mill to another at a rate faster than maidservants change their jobs. This gentleman from the MMC, during a career of 25 years, changed his employer 13 times. He roamed over the entire western and northern India. At 50 years of age he settled down as the factory manager of an upcoming textile mill in an out-of-the way location. There was no boss above him. The mill owner's visits were restricted to occasions like Dassera, Diwali, New Year's eve. In this position of all-in-all and above all, he did extremely well. He was better informed on the ideological aspects than the local mill union leader. His considerate approach towards juniors also worked wonders. Never before had the mill run as efficiently as under his stewardship. When he retired, the owner's son specially came to say goodbye and the union leader was in tears. He was then appointed as consultant to the mill.

Persons of your type normally have interests in diverse fields. They do better in hobby pursuits. It is always better for a person of your type to engage in social work where you will have more say as a man with a technical background. It can widen your field of contacts. This helps sometimes when you are in search of a job.

You can rise in the same organisation provided better opportunities come your way in the early stage of your employment. But this is a rare phenomenon.

A CASE STUDY

A person was employed in the R&D wing of a corporate sector company. He had the opportunity of being transferred to the production unit. He found himself getting restless at the slow pace of research work in the R&D wing. At the time of his transfer, his colleagues in the production unit were all of lesser calibre than him (the first constraint). His research background had helped him to develop a questioning attitude and non-conventional approach (the second constraint). Soon after his transfer, the company launched a new product. He contributed the most in overcoming the teething troubles (the third constraint). He out-smarted his colleagues and was soon promoted to a managerial position. Before he had made himself known as a person belonging to category C, he was out of the MMC.

A CASE STUDY

The veteran freedom fighter, astute politician and thinker, Shri Chakravarti Rajagopalachari, was a man of great intellect who often differed from the Mahatma in the heyday of the freedom struggle. Mahatma Gandhi, at that time, was all-in-all in the Indian National Congress. Rajaji, with his deep scholarship, his encyclopedic knowledge of Indian culture and outspokenness, often created storms within the organisation. However, the Mahatma was one of the best organizers of diverse personalities ever born and did not mind playing the role of ring master of a circus. He could contain Rajaji within the organisation and promoted him, so much so that it was Rajaji who took over the Governer General's post from Lord Mountbatten in the wake of independence. Rajaji was very outspoken and had an acid tongue. He often passed very sarcastic remarks. He had to separate himself from the ruling elite, especially Pt. Nehru, since the ring master was by then out of the picture. He must have caused Pt. Nehru to pass quite a few sleepless nights. Leaving behind his lifelong association with the INC, Rajaji, with other like-minded colleagues, formed a separate unit, the Svatantra party, in the post-independence years. He was the do-all and end-all of the party. The old man was never greatly troubled by the health hazards. He kept on writing books on the *Ramayana*, the *Mahabharata* and articles in newspapers, enlightening public opinion. Although Rajaji's name prominantly features in the annals of the freedom struggle, hardly any Congressman today ever refers to him. Nobody these days remembers that a political party such as the Svatantra party, was ever formed in India.

KNOW YOUR BOSS

A boss is like fire.Keep your distance, and
you lose warmth.Come close, you burn
your fingers. Identify the type of boss you
have to deal with.It will help you to decide
your distance from him or her.

One is free as a bird during one's educational career. Then the awful period of searching for a job starts. For the lucky ones, it comes to an end soon. It could happen that one has had to go through single, two-tier or three-tier interviews, depending on whether it is a private firm, a corporation or a governmental organisation. This also fixes the type of people you are going to encounter. The first or the second year of employment is spent in learning the job and getting acclimatised to the shopfloor modalities. You have not much voice in the whole affair. At the most you become a permanent employee of some organisation. Your contact with the boss, i.e. the person who decides your promotion and future or gives instructions to be followed, is nominal. Only after you become experienced and are given independent responsibilities, do your encounters with the boss become worth considering.

Let us understand the term BOSS. Its dictionary meaning is given as, 'a person who employs, superintends others; a foreman, a manager.'

This description of a person conveys some formal meaning. He is a person who exercises some authority and dominates over say production functions. However, there is one implicit meaning which almost all dictionaries have not mentioned. The author, however, does not claim to have seen  all dictionaries and his approach may not suit the lexicographer's method. But one encounters this particular function of a boss very often. Accordingly, the boss is a person who can overrule others, especially a junior's opinion, without giving any reason. The junior can be a recently employed supervisor on the shopfloor or the chief executive of a corporate sector company who can be overruled by the MD. Here again the dictionary meaning of the word 'overrule' can clarify the functions of the boss.

OVERRULE
1) To rule against or disallow the argument of a person
2) To rule or decide against (a plea, argument etc.)
3) To prevail over so as to change the purpose or action

This is a befitting description. All these meanings point to the real functions of the boss as you understand him. It is here, that the real conflicts of the situation start gaining ground and where you have to learn to accomodate.

A CASE STUDY

You have already planned some production schedule for the day. This was done in full consultation with the boss as per the daily or weekly schedule usually drawn up. You have already procured materials and allocated manpower. People are gearing up for the job. Suddenly you are summoned to the Boss's cabin. Even before you utter a single word you are asked to take up for production something other than what you have planned. It is on a top priority basis. Your attempts to explain certain problems regarding the reallocation of men and materials are curtly dismissed. You are not allowed to suggest that the same top priority job can be done a day after. You are overruled. You are left to deal by yourself with the uproar on the shopfloor. You think your boss could have left a note for you before leaving the factory the previous evening.

You go back to the shopfloor. The sudden rearrangement of materials creates transportation problems. The stores chap feels overburdened. He indicates that he may shed his burden at any moment. Shifting of men on the shopfloor results in the loudest uproar. You have to face it being a shopfloor supervisor. You may try to explain that an urgent job has to be taken on priority. This is more difficult when everybody knows that it could have been done the next day. To the changeover, their usual reaction is, 'Ye kampani me to sabhi urgent hota hai. Aja shadi karo aur kar bachcha chahiye. Ye nahi hoga sahab' (Tr : In this company everything is urgent. Marry today and deliver a child tomorrow. This won't happen sir.)

Though in the course of the day, things take the desired shape and the new production schedule is implemented, your acidity has risen by a few milligrams. Maybe your blood pressure has also risen by a few millimeters. As far as heart attack goes, its diagnosis still remains in the domain of heart specialists, to be interpreted from numerous graphs. It is better to remain ignorant about it. 'Ignorance is bliss' is very true in this case.

Let us look at the plant set up. Such situations of changing the job schedule and undertaking so called urgent jobs, are more frequent in plants producing product mixes in small amounts, say batch processes. In general the frequency of the sudden change of jobs varies in direct proportion to the number of products produced. It also varies in the square proportion to the boss's incompetence. An incompetent boss is often inconsiderate to his juniors. Even though he may know it beforehand, he may not reveal the change of schedule to his junior till the eleventh hour.

You can start distinguishing the good boss from the bad boss by his approach, as the former will always try to help his juniors. He will try to give them pre-intimation of such changes. In the event he forgets to inform you or leave a note on the previous evening, he will apologies. But a bad boss takes pleasure in not informing anyone and then looking on with amusement at the shopfloor *tamasha* which possibly he too has faced. He, as a sort, takes secret pleasure in revenge.

There are the techniques of planning, work scheduling and the much revered management methods of PERT/CPM. With the bad boss over one's head, implementing these techniques becomes a fruitless effort. If the boss has a fancy for these techniques, you have to break your head with them. At times you feel these techniques should be exported back to their country of origin i.e. the U.S.A.

There is one more important function where you will have to encounter the boss. It is while submitting the daily progress report or the log book. He is the one who has to do the firsthand assessment of your work. The following discussion is aimed at him.

A SITUATION TO AVOID

To start with, you should try to avoid a piquant situation as far as possible in which you have to report to your senior who too belongs to the MMC. These positions are those of senior foreman, senior executive officer and so on. He is generally a senior person in your cadre. He has spent more years in th e profession. He has usually acquired some skills like belittling juniors, especially the newcomers in the same cadre. He too is waiting for an opportunity to jump ahead. If he feels that you can elbow him aside and jump ahead of him, he will see to it that you are cut to size. This situation occurs in the beginning of one's career.

If you cannot avoid it, there are three ways to deal with this situation. For a short time, be really junior to him, take his firings lightly, even they be misplaced. Please him by accepting what he says. Boost his ego. Try to learn the tricks of the trade. You can be of real help to him. Thus, cultivate a good relationship with him. It always helps. Over the years he too has learned a few tricks of the trade. He will be pleased to share this information.

If he is not in the mood to be pleased, is too frustrated and trying to establish his own seniority, bypass him. Try to acquire a godfather in the higher echelons of the management. A senior person with this type of attitude in the MMC is a burden. Top people too are willing to communicate with fresh hands, maintaining, of course, a certain protocol. The cultivation of a godfather certainly nullifies the effect of this person.

The third alternative is never to continue for long under this situation. Either he moves out, to say another department or leaves the job (the least possible situation), or better, you move out.

TYPES OF BOSSES

Your boss changes with the sector of employment. This is a strange observation. As you go through the following text you will appreciate the sectorial classification. These are the—

1. Private sector boss
2. Corporate sector boss
3. Public sector boss

Further classification of bosses is given in the appropriate sections.

The Private Sector Boss

Let us not go into the legal details of what is the private sector. It would be a proprietary or partnership concern. In extreme cases it could even be a small public limited company. The private sector concern we are about to deal with is a single pole supported tent type. There is a single person who manages the whole show. His partners or shareholders are all sleeping partners. He is the only person who is responsible for the growth and prosperity of the concern. He is the do-all and end-all type of man.

It is in the private sector that one comes across the extreme types of bosses more often than in the other two sectors. You may be fortunate enough to work under a magnanimous individual. You may also end up under an extremely lousy person who has prospered out of sheer luck. They both come under the exceptional cases heading. With success, their idiosyncrasies too accentuate.

If you are lucky to join a concern in the early stage and manage to get along with the owner, then lady luck is also likely to smile on you. You become his right or left (whichever you think) hand and you too rise with him. Usually, these individuals believe in good and bad omens. In case he finds a rise in business after you join him, he may consider you to be a good omen and so on. Then you are one up. Instead of you adjusting to his idiosyncrasies, he will adjust to yours. You will be maintained as a happy employee at any cost. But this is a rare occurrence.

Your struggle to come up is more severe if you join an already established concern. By that time your boss has achieved some status. He is counted as somebody in his circle. He has learnt through experience to be survile with outsiders, unionised workers and government departments, financial institutions and so on. He is equally stern with his own MMC employees. His personality traits are more pronounced while dealing with his MMC employees. He can abuse you or threaten you with ouster on the next day. This he may not do in case you are found to be patiently listening to his harangue without batting an eyelid. He too needs to unload his blood pressure . If you have achieved this opportunity, you also have chances to rise in the organisation. But you have to thicken your skin to something tougher than that of a rhinoceros.

These types of abusive and ill mannered bosses are rarely appreciative of the good work you do. They are never pleased enough with your performance to award you some booty. They often do not know the worth of a man at the junior level.

Under these circumstances it should be in your mind that you cannot aspire to too much. If you are of category A, who can swallow any sort of harangue without batting an eyelid as stated earlier, then you are most suited for the job. But check whether this results in the suppression of anger or enmity towards him; you pass sleepless nights cursing him. Then you are harming yourself. There is no point in remaining a steady guy. Do not slog. Seek change of employment before you are attacked by one of these three ailments. Come out of the situation that can cause you any harm.

If for personal reasons such as family problems, education of children, locality and so on, you cannot leave the job, then develop the technique of keeping both ears open so that abusive harangue entering from one ear goes straight out the other without making an impact on the brain cells.

Category B and C cannot remain in such an organisation at all. The turnover of people in such organisations is high. Only category A can survive. It is only the survival instinct that helps them to rise up and up, adjusting with the boss. Do not go by the Darwinian dictum of the survival of the fittest. It is not even the half truth. While the great dinasaurs of a bygone era and the big cats (like tigers etc.) of the modern day have not survived or are facing extinction, the weak and the meek, like ants, cockroaches and wall lizards, have survived. It is the the weak and the meek who possess the capacity to adjust to the changed environment and survive.

If you are lucky enough to get a good, considerate boss who has built up his small or big empire, it is a pleasure to work. On realising that he is a good person, reciprocate in the same manner. Start taking an interest in the job right from the beginning. Try to learn as much as possible, both on the shopfloor as well as from books. Modernisation, automation and diversification are the catchwords of this age. You can discover new ideas and find these being appreciated and implemented without much delay. There is real joy in it. It is of more worth that the salary you get. Such bosses, on realising that the candidate is loyal to work and to the organisation, transfer their knowledge most willingly. It is also a pleasure to learn under their guidance. Your stay is fruitful for the organisation. There are fair chances to rise also. In case you seek a position elsewhere, this initiative from you enhances your chances in gaining a higher post. The initiative and knowledge automatically gets projected during any interview.

In a partnership concern where more than one partner is active in the day-to-day proceedings, unless

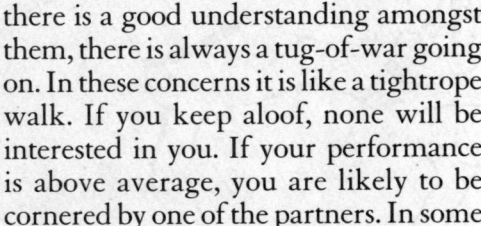

there is a good understanding amongst them, there is always a tug-of-war going on. In these concerns it is like a tightrope walk. If you keep aloof, none will be interested in you. If your performance is above average, you are likely to be cornered by one of the partners. In some cases you will get the opportunity to participate in a mediaeval type of court intrigue. At the end of such a coup in times past, if the plot succeeded, then one used to be awarded a knighthood. If it failed, however, the award was to be axed ruthlessly. In modern day operations, an unwanted partner is thrown out along with his minions.

Often, keeping aloof is not possible. Then you are suspected by both sides. But only the most powerful partner counts. Otherwise you are in the soup.

In a partnership concern, life is often a tug-of-war with you in the middle.

A CASE STUDY

A fresh graduate engineer was employed in a medium-sized partnership concern. He got along well with the young partner who was a lightweight and had got the partnership because of the sudden death of his father. This man had a consistent record of academic failure. He was sent for higher education to the U.S.A. by his father, where he successfully (?) completed a diploma in management. The engineer, however, was not fully aware of this partner's background except for the management diploma in the U.S.A. When the tug-of-war between the partners enjoined, financial matters came to the fore as usual. The first restrictions were placed on the workers' overtime. It was obvious. According to the Indian wage structure, overtime wages are double the normal wages.

The young partner once visited the factory premises late in the evening and saw two senior workers working overtime. He immediately ordered the engineer to withdraw these workers from the site. Being pally with him and not fully realising the implications, the engineer  stopped the furnace which contained the molten mass. Next day, when the heavyweight partner saw the mess inside the furnace, he was upset. A similar mess had occured earlier also. But this was a chance to teach a lesson to the fresh engineer as to who was the most powerful partner. He called in the engineer and without asking for any explanation, he gave a full account of the young partner's calibre and told him that as an engineer/supervisor, he should have used his discretion. He fired him left and right and then sacked him from the job.

Let us explore the third possibility. You have joined a partnership concern where the owner-partners have lost interest in running the show. They have already prepared the groundwork for closure. Because of governmental regulations they cannot do so. So not only the routine jobs but fresh employment also continues to take place. This you realise only after joining the concern. There prevails an atmosphere of anarchy and decadence. Nobody has any interest in production or output and so on. Legitimate and illegitimate means are employed by the owners to amass whatever possible from the assets and the credit. Those with few scruples can become part of the whole decadent culture. This is a temporary phase. Under these conditions it is better to quit the concern. It is better to be with a small upcoming concern than to flourish in a decaying big concern.

As a result of market competition and the growing realisation that you have to pay for talent, small concerns too, are offering better salaries these days. In a privately owned, flourishing concern, there are more chances of upword mobility. Your spirit may get dampened in the corporate sector or in big concerns.

THE CORPORATE SECTOR BOSS
In India, the corporate sector has grown very fast in recent years and has contributed immensely towards

the growth of the Indian economy. Many concerns pay their employees well, give them perks and are known as good paymasters. It is in these concerns that you seem to be able to earn that little bit more in order to save something and enjoy life in today's inflationary world. However, you may soon realise that the money you have earned and saved has lost its value under the pressure of sky rocketing inflation.

The Government of India has adopted the mixed economy model which received a further boost after the policy of liberalisation was adopted. Many family concerns have now grown into corporate sector leaders. They went to the public for funds by issuing shares. They formed boards of directors where usually well known names featured. A sort of anonimity has occured at the top. The direct contact of owners with employees has been lost. An elaborate hierarchy in the management cadre has developed. As a result, many administrative hurdles have cropped up. In a proprietory concern, all the decisions remain with the owner. He can also do good to you if he wishes. In the corporate sector this cannot be done directly. The path towards achievement remains full of hurdles. This is no good for the MMC.

A CASE STUDY

An engineer was employed in a corporate sector company as a trainee supervisor. During his training period he proved to be a very good supervisor. Not only his immediate boss but his supervisors too, were

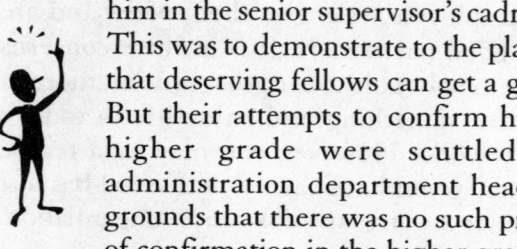

pleased with his performance. They agreed to confirm him in the senior supervisor's cadre directly. This was to demonstrate to the plant people that deserving fellows can get a good start. But their attempts to confirm him in the higher grade were scuttled by the administration department head, on the grounds that there was no such precedence of confirmation in the higher grade. In the company statute book there was no provision for the rewarding of such an outstanding performance in the non-managerial cadre.

In the meanwhile, the boss had made known his intentions to others in the plant, in good faith. But at the time of confirmation, the engineer, was confirmed in the regular cadre only. This, of course, reduced his enthusiasm. He also became an object of sarcastic amusement for his colleagues. Unable to bear the brunt and humiliation of being called a *chamcha* (sychophant) of the *sahab*, he left the job.

It is normally understood that in the private-corporate sector emphasis is placed on accountability. These sectors pay higher salaries and extract more work. There is an additional price tag attached to the job. There are production incentives for the workers and the MMC also in some cases. But performance is never tension free. The conflicting pursuits of workers and management has, in fact, led to distortion in the duties of the MMC. MMC's have to face the music from both sides.

There is yet another important aspect. It is a power game at the company directors' level. It is played basically on ethnic lines. Although the old jargon of castism is outdated nowadays, it is very likely that your boss  is occupying his seat because he belongs to the same ethnic group as one of the directors. You too may cross over the MMC barrier and occupy the managerial position for the same simple reason. So, after joining the company, go through the list of directors. Know their ethnic backgrounds. Keep aneye on the motion of people rising upwards. Maybe somebody from the top is also keeping an eye on you.

THE COMPETANT BOSS

You are likely to encounter this type of boss more often in the corporate sector. That is why the performance of the private/corporate sector is better than the public sector. If your boss is competent, you come to know it quickly. It does not take a long time to judge such a person. Your colleagues may give their own version of his competence. You too come to know whether you are competent for the job. If you are not competent, then as long as your boss is on your head, you cannot aspire to rise. At the same time as long as you are not a nuisance to anybody, none will bother you. If you do not realise your capacity and aspire for promotion and so on, you start bothering yourself. The attack of the threesome is imminent.

If you too are competent and need a little training and guidance of some sort, then working under a competent boss is really a very good opportunity.

There is, however, a big IF. Though competent, if your boss is highly biased due to certain considérations such as ethnic or personal rapport and determined to favour your colleague for the same consideration, then you are doubly troubled. You have to give a far superior performance. Then you have landed yourself in greater trouble and the attack of the threesome occurs at a quicker pace.

Normally, competent people like other competent people. Then they are ready to share their experiences with their juniors. It is interesting to learn how they manage the operations. A competent person in a deserving position in most cases transcends petty ethnic and personal considerations. He judges the performance of his juniors more objectively. In such a case you have to exploit the opportunity. You can literally chart your way upwards. Your attitude then should be to help your boss to rise in the hierarchy. He will take you along with him , even if he changes his job for better chances to rise. Achievements and promotions do not come in isolation. Every boss too desires and needs co-operation from his juniors and more so from those who are competent and willing.

Once you have identified that your boss is really competent for the position he is occupying, open up with him. He too will like it. Try to learn from him, discuss your drawbacks, get the corrective measures from him and improve your performance. None in this world can come up without taking risks and committing mistakes. You too will commit them. You can correct yourself with the help of your boss. Your commitment to your work can be better appreciated by your boss. You are left with fewer conflicts. If you think you are faithfully and efficiently discharging your duties, it is no great thing. You are being paid for that. But you are expected to do something more. You can diversify your work from the routine job you are doing. Initiative on your part can fetch you better results. The boss is bound to note it. As stated earlier, even if he isbiased, your performance will reduce its intensity and for you it may dissappear.

While diversifying your interests and work areas, try to understand the needs of your boss. He needs your help not only for the shopfloor jobs but for many other things in order to run the show smoothly. There are always problems concerning men, materials and machines. Nobody can be perfect in all these spheres. You can make up for his shortcomings. Try to acquire more competence and knowledge in the areas he is lagging in, to the extent that your boss starts relying on you. That makes for a team. Teamwork always results in better performance.

Once the area of diversification has been identified, go on learning about it so that your boss too acknowledges your competence for the newly acquired skill. Your boss who is competent for the post he is occupying may have reached his maximum level of competence. His boss too notes it and is on the lookout for somebody who makes up his deficiency. Then your chances for rising higher are greater. But take precautions. Do not let your boss feel threatened because of your performance. In that case there might be a few conflicting situations. But the work, the shopfloor jobs, have to be completed in unison. This is a case of marginal competence.

A simple method can be devised to work under a marginally competent boss. First judge for yourself that the boss has reached his maximum level of competence. Here your own judgement of his performance becomes crucial. Let there be no mistake. So do not hurry. Continue to learn, interact and perform better. On judging it, do not take to him the problems that he cannot solve. Rather, take to him the problems that he can solve and give him due credit. Try to solve the other problems yourself and keep on making a note of these in your log book or performance track record. Since you are not taking to him the prblems he cannot solve, he too feels relieved. Your performance can then be noted by his boss, who otherwise was required to make up for your boss's deficiency. Then you have fair chances to overstep your boss. Positive and healthy competition always proves to be good for any organisation.

A CASE STUDY

A technically competent senior supervisor was promoted to a managerial position. In his position, apart from looking after production, he was required to look into the product allocation for sale and materials management. Whenever there was a problem on the shopfloor, he would come running to the plant and see to it that the problem was solved. He thus spent more time on the shopfloor. His work on product allocation and materials management thus started suffering. After some time, virtual anarchy reigned on the shopfloor on account of shortfall of materials. Here his erstwhile colleague came to his help out of friendship and set the production schedule right. At the same time, he was wise enough to seek the guidance of the boss on technical problems which kept his boss happy. This performance was noted by the higher ups. The boss too was pleased about the help he received and this junior man's case was strongly recommended. Not surprisingly, he soon superseded the erstwhile boss.

THE INCOMPETANT BOSS

While the levels of competence can be identified, there are no levels of incompetence. A person gets into a higher but undeserved position on account of various considerations. The first and foremost being his seniority in the organisation. Second being considerations other than his competence. Here ethnic or personal considerations other than his competence come into the picture. Thirdly, the man may be directly recruited for a position where his performance cannot be judged.

Seniority is a frequently observed norm for promotion. This is more so in the case of a person who is about to retire after having put in several years in the MMC. Private managements too become considerate and promote such senior citizens to locations where they need to be least effective. They too know and are happy to carry on for a year or two before retirement. If you have such a boss, try to remain in his good books. He is a harmless person. Having spent years in the organisation and the very fact that the management has become considerate towards him, indicates that he has good rapport with the higher ups. Being in his good books helps on both fronts. Over the years he has usually developed good relations with workers and they too have a soft corner for him. Your good relations with him can be of help in critical times. When retiring, he can speak well of you to the management.

If a new recruit in the managerial position proves to be incompetent, there are few chances of his remaining in the same position. But there could be other compelling reasons for the management to continue with him. In that case, such a person will try to pass on his incompetence to his juniors and can inflict harm to them if he is of a vengeful nature. Guard against this type of man. Do not enter into conflict with him unless you have backing from the higher ups. If he is leaving the organisation, let him do the least harm to you. But if he is to continue, follow the same treatment as outlined earlier in the case of the marginally competent boss.

The real conflicting situation arises when your boss has acquired the position because of some favour done to him for reasons other than technical. This boss is very conscious of this consideration. He is always on the lookout to make his presence felt. He even tries to interfere in routine decisions you normally take on the shopfloor. He also keeps shelving certain important decisions because of lack of confidence. It is very difficult to convince such a boss about the right approach. He is bent on not being convinced. Constant interference from such a boss is a real headache. Often he lands you in trouble by placing the responsibility of his wrong decisions onto you. This kills one's initiative. If you are ambitious then you become more prone to attack by the three health hazards. Again, in this case, do not enter into conflict with the boss. Adopt the policy of wait and watch. Sooner or later his incompetence is bound to be exposed and will be known to those who decided to promote him for whatever considerations.

To deal with such a boss, you have to be a really astute person or rather, a politician. The first and foremost thing to remember is not to tell the boss about his incompetence. In most cases he already knows it. Remember that he is vested with power, rather an extra constitutional power, so he can inflict more harm. There are always people around you to exploit the situation of your conflict with the boss. They enjoy seeing you in real trouble.

If you belong to category A, you can easily become friendly with him. In fact, he needs all such people.

In addition, if you are competent yourself for the job, it is a favourable situation for you.

For people belonging to categories B and C, it is better to remain at arms distance from such a boss. Try to make it a point not to associate with his decisions. The usual way to give him credit or discredit for the interfering instructions he gives you, is to mention these in the logbook and write API. At the time of conflicting and wrongly implemented decisions, you can point out to the upper bosses that you did not agree with him but followed the instructions. That keeps him in a tight position and at hands distance from you too. Do not hope to get any reward under this situation. So wait and watch. Situations always change with time, sometimes for the better and sometimes maybe for the worse.

A CASE STUDY

A manager was newly appointed in a multinational corporate sector giant. There were two main considerations. First, a close relative of his was the chief secretary in the concerned department at the Centre. The second, was that a distant relative of his was on the board of directors. Even the relative on the board of directors consented to his recruitment only after confirming his connection in Delhi. On being appointed to this position, he became intoxicated by the power he commanded. He started dictating terms on all and sundry issues and went on failing. As a result, he did not get cooperation from his subordinates. The workers went on strike because of his approach and with the mute consent of his juniors. Finally, he started getting a battering from his subordinates. Within two years of his appointment, he was thoroughly exposed. As he could not be removed,  he was shunted to some unimportant project which mattered very little for the company. The evil influence he inflicted on the unit took years to heal.

Incompetent bosses of the scheming type are real dangers. They often owe their position to this quality and thrive in an atmosphere of decadence. If you know that you too possess the same quality, then you can be apart of the whole and rip off the benefits. But do not take the risk if you are not a good plotter and schemer.

Having an utterly incompetent boss is a transient phase in the corporate sector. Either the boss goes or the company goes. Therefore, patience only pays in this case.

THE PUBLIC SECTOR BOSS

Employment in this sector is the safest and has the least botherations. Anybody in our country will say that the overall performance of the public sector, entirely funded by the government, is no good and often dismal, and leaves much to be desired. A few years ago, public sector employees received comparatively 65% lower payments and the private sector offered attractive remunerations and perks. Hence, the private sector attracted talented young people. Of late, things have changed. The public sector also offers good salaries with perks like spacious accomodation, public schooling for the children, occasional foreign jaunts for new projects, and so on. At the same time, there is no corresponding pressure to perform. This has resulted in some talented young men seeking employment in the public sector and sticking there till retirement. This has not resulted in improved performance in most cases. On the contrary, the talent of many of these young men was not utilized. It either rusted or was directed towards some undesirable activities. Some returned to the private sector. Many of the talented men, who remained behind, refused to take for granted the supremacy of the bureaucracy. As a result, there was tussle between the I.A. S. cadre bosses imposed on them and these people. And the new jargon of bureaucracy vs technocracy was added to the English language. In the end, the government yielded. The powers of the chief engineers, the chairmen of the public sector units and so on, were put on par with IAS officers of the secretary level. Over the years, the government services and the public sectors have become sanctuaries mainly for those who like to lead peaceful lives. Occasional outbursts from the political masters results in suffering of some individual at the higher echelons. On the whole, the situation has remained more or less the same before and after the pay scale revision and the placement of a technocrat in place of a bureaucrat.

The factors that are responsible for the much to be desired performances of the PSUS, also determine the type of bosses one can encounter. Apart from the competent boss, there are three types of bosses in the public sector.

You are likely to encounter an incompetent boss more often in the PSUS. Your boss may have acquired his position due to three main reasons. The first and foremost being seniority, the date and hour of joining duty. Secondly, he may have the right connections either in the political or bureaucratic circles of the corresponding ministry. Thus, either he has a powerful local politician supporting him or some influential officer in Delhi is taking care of his interests. The third important reason could be that your boss belongs to the category of SC/ST candidature and is thus promoted through the governmental quota for such promotions. One needs to adopt a different approach for these bosses.

One of the major problems one is likely to face in a PSU is inquiry by some commission about some scandal or the other, or about some real or false mistake.

The confidential reports are annually written by your boss. His good remarks may not be of help to you, but his bad remarks can and always will come in the way of promotions. Your boss may not be in a position to help you to rise, but he can always implicate you in the same scandal or fraud he is involved in. He can issue you a suspension notice.

These notices can be withdrawn by applying pulls at the appropriate locations but your life is made miserable. With so many upheavals and scandals rocking the country, implicating persons from the prime minister to the local *gram panchayat surpanch*, it is in fact, a tightrope walk in the PSU's, not to get involved in any type of scandal.

There is a panacea for all this. As soon as you get your confirmation letter, try to keep aloof from all official or unofficial activities. Do your regular duty as expected. Project your aloofness by calling everybody thief, i.e. *sab chor hai*, but refrain from openly criticising your boss or any person or his connections. Build up your image as a man with least nuisance value. Having done it, if you are technically competent and ready to share a little of the credit with your boss, you have fair chances to rise higher. Your annual confidential reports then carry no adverse remarks. These too can be officially expunged as per the government procedure. This procedure is again a tedious and time consuming affair. So prevention is better than cure.

Your real test in PSUs lies in keeping aloof from all the politics going round. While dealing with a competent boss, it does need great effort to meet his expectations. But this is technical in nature, related to the job. A competent MMC can manage it. The problem arises only when the boss is incompetent. In PSUs it is necessary to know the background of your boss and how he reached this position. That will determine your course of action.

BOSS BECAUSE OF SENIORITY

Though incompetent, if your boss has received promotion to the higher post through seniority, then be sure that he had to wait in the queue for long years. Unless he is vengeful by nature, he is considerate towards his juniors. If he finds in you what he wants, he will always be with you. Most of his more dominating colleagues must have superseded him. So there is an inbuilt aversion in him to the dominating traits in your approach to him. So to start with, be soft spoken. Show a little human consideration by not letting him down. This type of suggestion is necessary because there is a tendency to do otherwise, since you know all about his incompetence. This will help him to overcome his inferiority complex while dealing with you.

There are very few occasions in the PSUs for developing conflict with the boss on technical matters. In these matters you can politely differ with him. Put your views on paper in clear terms and officially forward the paper to him. Let the decision remain with him. In this case you have performed your solemn duty to make him aware of the pros and cons. While sending the note, do not make it personal. Make it a general note so that he too can put his learned remarks on it and pass it on to his superior. Thus the buck is passed on and on. PSUS have no tradition of firm decision making at lower levels. There is as yet no Roosevelt employed with any of these PSUs who affirms 'the buck stops here'.

All is well till the activity continues from the last page to the current page. If some problem arises, the blame will trickle down from the top to your level and maybe to you in person. An inquiry committee is set up. When the committee calls you for questioning, you can produce the duplicate of the letter you had given your boss with due acknowledgement from his secretary or steno. Scribblings on paper under these circumstances can do or undo your career. If things go well, your boss will certainly come back to you next time for consultation. Oblige him. That helps to get better CRs at the year end.

Apart from the regular pay revision demands and work-to-rule or *bandh* activities by unions, occasional conflicts arise in PSUs or government departments when a new boss joins as the head of the institution or some politician holding your department ministry post openly criticises your unit in particular in Parliament and it gets published in the newspapers.

As soon as a new head joins the organisation and takes over from the previous man who mostly retires, he delivers a general address to all the employees. He, as usual, harps on accountability, production rise and efficiency. The same thing could happen when a central government minister visits your plant and delivers a sermon. The tide percolates down to you within a short time in the form of circulars and notes. You have to raise production and minimise waste. You are aware of a new drive by the head of the institution. Workers too start showing some change, for the sake of change. The top brass is found to take a round of the shopfloor and is occasionally observed talking to the union leaders. This tide continues till everybody who matters has assessed the new top man, his connections in NEW DELHI, and possible opportunities for rising or transfer. Under these circumstances, you too are temporarily pressurised by your immediate boss to show more production. The only hitch that holds back all these drives being getting the work done from the permanent government employees on the shopfloor. They do not get pressurised. They have solid union coverage, the show processes a of governmental inquiries and labour favouring laws. So you have to work it out on a personal level. If you have good rapport with good workers, they will produce a little more than usual. That you can show as rise in production and make it  known in the places where it matters. Then you may get a chance to rise and supersede your boss also. If it is not possible, then calm yourself. This tide is never a permanent feature. To save yourself and your boss, prepare a statement pointing to materials mismanagement, the short supply of raw materials in time, technical problems of full capacity production and so on. Point out in clear terms why it is not possible to rise above the present capacity. Do not blame any specific department or person. That creates a problem. Also give a suggestion or two for improving the system and sent the note to your boss for forwarding to the higher ups. Your boss is pleased. You have reduced his burden. These tides subside. Production continues from the last page onwards as usual. It is patience that can keep you away from the health hazards. As stated in the *Ishopanishad*, the ancient text, there is pleasure in sacrifice—*ten tyakten bhunjithah*.

So sacrifice a bit of credit or use a bit of your writing skill for your boss. If you try to protect your boss by seniority, your CR at the end of the year will be better. That is what matters in a government organisation or in PSUs.

Boss Because of Political or Bureaucratic Connections

In the private as well as corporate sectors, it is considered natural that the son of somebody will also be somebody unless he is utterly useless. Thus the son of the MD of a private limited company has to end up being MD of the same company in most cases. The son takes the responsibility and is groomed for it. The son thus groomed acquires ability and magnanimity to carry on the job of Papa gracefully. That's the way scions of the Indian industry have built their empires over the last three generations. But in the PSUs, if your boss has acquired his position because of his appropriate connections in political or bureaucratic circles, then he is likely to become a dangerous species. Thriving on unsavoury means, he invariably develops similar traits. He feels guilty in mind but as a reaction and psychological counter measure, he becomes vengeful. If he is competent, then it is very difficult to deal with him. He is always suspicious. If he is corrupt in addition, it becomes a tightrope walk to deal with such a boss. Better keep away. For persons not belonging to category A, he is difficult to deal with. One has to be scheming enough to keep him pleased. But then you are losing your self esteem and compromising. Possibly you have to be part of the corrupt clout. You have to decide. There is no point in delivering sermons. You cannot prevent corruption in the prevailing politicoeconomic system in India. At the MMC level there is not much scope for directly indulging in commission-gift business.

This type of influence-oriented boss would like to see things on shopfloor going smoothly. Give him time to breath for himself. Try not to harbour grudges against him. Don't forget that the majority of PSU employees, including yourself, will be happy to exploit such a powerful connection. Try not to foment trouble for him. Wait and watch. He himself will call for trouble. Avoid clashes with him. Unless you too have proper connections elsewhere. By clashing with him you will harm yourself. Take it as your lot. Do not think of changing your job if you and your family are accustomed to the pesceful life in a PSU campus. As such, there is no question of accountability. But in the outside world the rat race and many other problems in day-to-day life escalate mental tensions. This invites early attack by the threesome. Save your skin and pull on. On account of his proper connections your boss may be pulled further upwards or he loses his power with the decline in power of his political master.

It is also a common observation that the wife of such a person is extra conscious of his connections and particularly if the connection is from her side. Do not let your family interfere with this. This invariably leads to intrafamily tensions. These in turn reflect onto your shopfloor dealings. Tell your wife not to interact much. Thus, you keep trouble away from you and your family as well.

Unless your boss is sure that you are in no way harmful for him, he will not relish your taking extra interest in the job. Sometimes your boss gets implicated in some production disturbance, scandal or newspaper report on corruption. Under these conditions, go on long leave, preferably on medical leave. As such, the government jobs offer a good number of days of sick leave. Accumulate them to be utilized at the critical time. You also get a chance to expose your boss, showing him his real position and cutting him down to size. After such an incident, bypass him. Establish rapport with his boss and improve your chances to rise. But confirm that he too is not influence-oriented like your boss.

A Case Study
A capable MMC employed with a PSU, found himself transferred one fine morning to a section

where the boss was known to have very strong connections in the state capital. For the time being he kept his cool. He neither pooh-poohed his boss nor tried to outsmart him. He got instructions in writing from the boss as far as possible. One afternoon, he got a note from his boss asking him to make some changes in the production schedule. It could not be done easily. It would have created some technical problems on the shopfloor. He made inquiries and realised that the new schedule was the brainchild of his boss only. As such, the boss could have called him and found out from him the problems he was going to face. Before leaving the factory premises, he left a short note for the boss, narrating the difficulties in implementation. He went on short leave and did not report back. The boss went ahead with his brain child. It was a filmsy modificatio. It was not acceptable to the workers who created an uproar. The boss had exposed himself. After resuming duty, he pointed out to the boss his note outlining the difficulties. The employee then passed on the same note to higher ups. In due course the boss was shunted aside and the employee started reporting directly to the boss's boss with clear written instructions. His patience in waiting till his boss exposed himself payed off.

BOSS BECAUSE OF RESERVED SEATS

Reservations for backward class candidates at almost all levels of government service is a major decision willingly taken by all the citizens of India. It has constitutional support. The founding fathers of the constitution had definite foresight in taking this far-reaching decision. Accordingly, the quota system was devised for the recruitment of candidates from the SC/ST strata. These days the quota changes according to the political expediency of the ruling party at the centre or at the state level.

It is very likely that you will find a junior colleague belonging to one of these groups superseding you. He becomes your boss. He is invariably of inferior calibre. It certainly creates a murmer in your heart. Take it for granted. It is bound to happen these days. If you come from a higher caste, think that you are repaying the price of the inhuman treatment given by your ancestors to the ancestors of your boss. Realise that in this age, leading towards an egalitarian society, people from the backward classes need and deserve special promotions and facilities. Understand this and your mental conflict is reduced by fifty percent. On the social level you have accepted the correct attitude.

Now comes personal level dealing. It is a tricky job to deal with him since he may belong to the same department and has been your junior at some time. On suddenly finding him in a superior position, you are in a defiant mood. The earlier you reconcile yourself to the situation, the better for your health. It is the experience of many superseded employees that such bosses are eager to show off their ability and are also interested in making a fast buck. They are also prone to making

mistakes. The higher bosses too expect it to happen. They too find themselves helpless.

If this SC/ST boss is a sober man who realises his deficiency and does not carry the burden of a past history, he can be easily dealt with. In fact, maturity on his part can help you both. If he is ready to learn, understand and improve his capability, cooperate with him. Help him to come up to the level of competence required for the job. By cooperating with him you have done service to society and the nation. By adopting such an attitude you have contributed your share towards amilioration of social disparity. You can feel satisfied. In some cases this cooperation results in a steady friendship and even family relationships.

In many cases, however, this boss carries with him old grievances. He treats his colleagues from the upper classes very badly. He behaves as if he is taking revenge for the treatment given to his forefathers. He passes snide remarks about their social status. He burdens them with a heavy workload to test their ability and if not completed in the given time, he harps on their inability and social status. Soon, such bosses become unpopular. Their unpopularity is noted by the seniors and they are shunted aside. Juniors then bypass them and start reporting to those who matter and continue to work. These bosses do not get cooperation from their colleagues, feel isolated and are transferred to the departments where they are least bothersome. Under these circunstances it is better to soothe yourself with the feeling that many others are also sailing in the same boat. You may also tell your boss your feelings about the situation. You may ask him, why you should be held responsible for the misdeeds of your forefathers as long as he is getting the promotion, pay package and social status as well? He has to command respect rather than demanding it.

A Case Study

A scheduled caste person was promoted to a managerial position superseding many senior colleagues from the upper castes. This young chap was bright compared to others and became over confident. He always taunted his upper caste colleagues. He used to burden them with extra workload, which had no relevance to the immediate job. An old colleague from the upper caste took up the challenge. He organized the work allotted to him within the stipulated period and went to report back to his boss. As used to happen, the boss would not offer him a seat. He reported to the boss that all the work was accomplished and answered his queries. Now the boss could not say any derogatory words. Picking this opportunity, he fired the boss left and right. As an elderly person, he could have been offered a seat. By adopting such a vengeful attitude, not only did the boss harm himself but society as a whole. He was losing goodwill for his caste brethren. It is such atrocious behaviour that has led to widespread resentment against reservations. It would be in fact beneficial for a person of his type to leave behind old grievances, fully utilize the facilities available for improving his own competence and hence further the common lot of his caste.

Other colleagues of the old man were listening to the conversation from outside the cabin. They too had suffered at the hands of this boss. When the conversation inside the cabin stopped, they went in one by one and uttered only one sentence, that they fully agreed with their senior colleague. The boss was dumbfounded. He realised the mass resentment against himself and it could result in his being transferred to a nondescript post. He called the senior colleague back to his cabin, apologised and sought his cooperation. From then onwards, he changed his behaviour. Now he has risen much higher and is rated highly by his colleagues.

It is likely that your boss is too immature. Even after realising that, he is not able to get cooperation from his colleagues he continues to be adamant. When you cannot tolerate him, then lookout for a transfer to some other section. In government departments such inter-departmental transfers are routine.

If the boss is competent, then deal with him as if you would deal with a normal competent boss. By the time he has achieved competence he has shed the burden of historic grievances.

A Few Last Words

The types of bosses dealt with in this chapter do not make up all the types. However, the basic tendency in human beings to dominate and show off power is to be understood. You too would like to exercise power. So look at yourself. That helps to reduce tension.

Any boss is like fire. Keeping away too much is losing the warmth. Going too near is to risk burning your fingers.

A proper and constructive attitude towards the functioning of the PSU machinery, clear communication of technical problems to your boss, taking his orders in the right spirit and, beyond a certain point, shedding the responsibility of decision making, transferring it to your boss, helps to keep oneself calm.

As such the work load in this sector is less. The government too looks at this sector as an employment shop with no guarentee of proportional returns. So there is not enough work, specially at the lower echelons. This invariably leads to the so-called NO WORK SYNDROME. And you know very well what it is. For all those employed in the public sector and who are interested in keeping themselves fit, should not succumb to this no work syndrome. It is always better to keep oneself fruitfully busy. It could be by doing your duty efficiently and faithfully or by doing some constructive activity. It is peace of mind, a tension-free evening with the family and good habits like taking long walk, regular exercise, reading, engaging in a fruitful hobby, some genuine type of social work and leisurely spending time with good friends, that keep the three ailments away.

DEALING WITH THE WORKERS

Workers are an amorphous lot.
Better deal with them as individuals with
known traits. Escalating problems with
workers can cause unnecessary hurdles
in your passage upwards.

You are a shopfloor man in the MMC. You can, for a while, forget the boss, but the workers are your constant companions. They too know this and therefore need to be given due thought while you deal with them.

Depending on the location, type of sector and so on, you may have to work with unionised or non-unionised workers. All of them, in their heart of hearts, know your powerless position. What, at the most you can do is to take their complaints to the boss and no further. You have to reduce these as well. Secondly, your responsibility is also limited. You are not an order passing and coordinating agency.

When it comes to dealing with workers, one has to keep in mind that workers as a group have an amorphous identity. You have also to deal with individual workers. As long as you are able to keep the problem of dealing with him at an individual level, it gives no tension. But if you allow it to escalate, and go beyond the shopfloor to either the union or the boss, it starts reflecting on you.

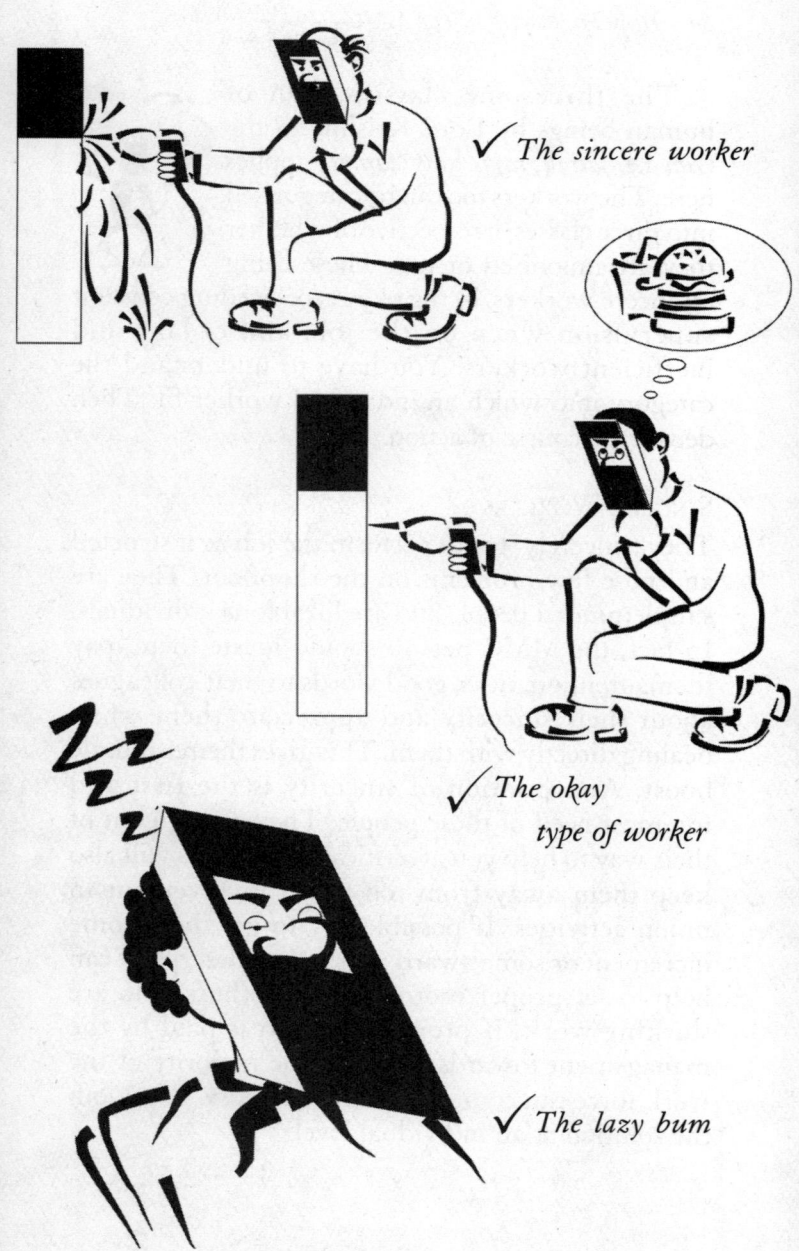

✓ *The sincere worker*

✓ *The okay type of worker*

✓ *The lazy bum*

The threesome classification of human beings by Lord Krishna in the *Gita* i.e. *satvik*, *rajas* and *tamas* applies here. The workers too can be categorised into three classes, irrespective of whether they are unionised or not. These being a) sincere workers, b) the okay type needing constant supervision when on the job, and c) lazy and inefficient workers. You have to understand the category into which an individual worker fits. Then decide the course of action.

SINCERE WORKERS

They sincerely try to perform the job as instructed and pose few problems on the shopfloor. They are simpleminded people and are lovable as individuals. In fact, the MMC person should locate them, pay them attention, utter good words to their colleagues about their sincerity and appreciate them while dealing directly with them. This gives them a morale boost. Appreciation of sincerity is the first and foremost need of these people. They may go out of their way to help you at critical times. This will also keep them away from too much involvement in union activities. If possible, try to get them some increment or some award which they deserve. It can help to set proper motivation for others who are shirking work. If proper attention is paid by the management towards workers, the majority of the work force can come under this category. Work out the solution at an individual level.

THE OKAY TYPE OF WORKERS

They work but do not put in their full efforts. They need constant attention when on the shopfloor. They cannot concentrate. Hence, to be safe, keep track of their work lest they commit mistakes. Occasional raising of the voice helps to keep them on the right track. Call them aside and point out their failures. At the same time, appreciate a good job whenever done. This helps them to be motivated. Some workers of this type already have a track record of committing blunders periodically. Guard against that because the blame of these blunders will always be passed on to you.

 Sometime, even a sincere worker becomes like this. Understand then that there is certain problems with him. Talk to him. If it is due to a personal family problem, try to slove it by giving good guidance. He will appreciate it and come back to his normal sincerity. Dealing with both these types of workers with human consideration, can always help you to be like by them. they offer least resistance in the normal course of working. This also gives you much less tension and keeps the health hazards away.

THE LAZY BUMS

They are the lazy dregs. They are known to everybody to be so. They are always hunting for an opportunity to keep away from work. During night shifts, they often try to run away and take a nap. They are least bothered by any scolding and cannot be motivated to improve. They are usually the fellows who get easily trapped by union leaders of the scheming type. They are always in the forefront to air their grievances against the MMC to the management.

These workers should be identified from the beginning. They should be isolated and kept under tension by catching them redhanded, given notice, faced with inquiries and so on. Then you can remain tension free. Or else they start giving you tension. Excepting some of the union leaders, they usually receive no backing from the workers. Any strict action taken against them will be consented to by fellow workers although not openly. For some known or unknown reason, they get confirmed in service and then it becomes difficult to remove them. So, be strict with these types. Keep accumulating a record of their failures which can come to your help or the help of the management whenever strict action is necessary.

Some of these types of workers soon become militant union leaders. They grow in stature. They start talking directly to the boss. The bosses too become victims. Under these circumstances, keep aloof. Do not quarrel. It is for the management to take action against them. If such a fellow has strong political or union backing, he cannot be removed. You have to keep on tolerating him like a vagabond son. Accept it. Your boss too will not enquire into

his whereabouts. Too many such workers
in any organisation invariably leads to its
fall. Closure of many industrial units due
to so-called labour unrest, is on account
of such workers not being kept under
strict control and being allowed to grow
in numbers.

A few words about union activity. Unionism is a
part and parcel of the work ethos now. The ideology
in the '70s has given way to gross materialism in every
field of activity. Unions too, are no exception. The
labour laws, too much in favour of labour, have created
problems for management all over the country. As a
member of the MMC, you do not feature in this grand
design. While dealing with workers of the three types
outlined above, the first two types can also turn into
union leaders. If they develop antagonistic attitudes
towards you in particular, then look at yourself.
Identify the category to which you belong and accept
it as a fait accompli. Remember you cannot become
an instrument in improving labour and management
relations. The union leaders too have become
professionals and work out their equations with the
management directly.

The union leaders keep talking of the capitalist
class exploiting the working class. But these are all
slogans. The gullible workers get carried away by
this talk and agree to unreasonable demands through
the union. The class war attitude of the unions against
management has stalled the labour force in our
country from becoming producers themselves. The

labourers and their leaders cannot put themselves into the shoes of the management. There is hardly any instance in industry where the workers or the labour leaders have taken over from the management and run the unit more efficiently.

It is production that creates wealth. The more the labourers avoid it, the poorer they become. To keep your conscience clear, do not aggravate the union problem to the extent of leading to the closure of the unit. There are cases when the adamant attitude of the MMCs supported by management, have led to the closure of units, thereby depriving many uninvolved and needy people of their livelihood. Your ineptitude in dealing with workers by escalating tensions can come in the way of your upward mobility.

GIVING A PIECE OF YOUR
MIND TO YOUR BOSS

*Sometimes you have to give a piece of
your mind to your most loving wife.
So do not shirk giving it to your boss.
He too needs it. But bide an opportune
time for the appropriate impact.*

Giving a piece of your mind to your boss is a crucial operation and you have to perform it carefully. Although there are three types of sectors where one has to deal with bosses, in PSUs the ambience is the most lethargic. Most times you just shed the burden by way of giving a written note, things rarely come to an impasse. In the private and corporate sector, where performance of an MMC candidate is judged critically, there are more occasions for shedding the load on one's mind. A piece of your mind needs to be given to an incompetent boss and not to the competent one. The very fact that you have not allowed any situation to flare up between him and you shows that you are mature enough to tolerate it. Either your boss has not realised his shortcomings or he has taken you for granted. You have to carefully plan to execute the operation. If you do not shed the load on your mind, you start developing problems with yourself. You thereby invite attack from these three health enemies within.

The plan of action given below is a broad guideline. It is for you to put the details in according to the situation prevailing in your organisation.

The Plan of Execution

 Decide on a period of say one or two months from that of your decision to give a piece of your mind to your boss. Over that period, keep a detailed record of your boss's failures, instance by instance. Also give a possible alternative to overcome the situation. Do not let your colleagues know your decision and also do not show over anxiety to note the boss's failures. Restrict these instances only to yourself and to your shift.

Be sincere in your work and perform your duty properly. He should not get any opportunity to point a finger at you.

Do not openly discuss his failure on the shopfloor or pass any remark. Such remarks get circulated to the upper echelons. It is undesirable at this juncture.

After having accumulated a few such instances, wait for an opportunity when your boss calls you for an individual meeting. If he is not in the habit of doing so, take a prior appointment with him. Select a day when there are no problems on the shopfloor. Otherwise, he can cut you off in the middle of the talk and send you back to the shopfloor and put you in a corner. Do not select the days prior to his meeting with his bosses or board of directors meeting. The selection of a proper day and a proper time is crucial.

And no readymade formula can be given to select it. You are the best judge.

Once it is ensured, get a hint about his mood if possible from his secretary or a colleague who has just met him. Seek his permission. State that you want to talk to him about production – plant problems and if he agrees, then only go ahead.

On his agreeing to talk to you, thank him. Appreciate his willingness to spare the time and then open up. Discuss the failures instance by instance. Do not mince words in pointing out his shortcomings. Also point out the help you had either offered or could have offered if he had consulted you. Because you are a shopfloor man you know better where the shoe pinches. Take each of his decisions, analyse its pros and cons. If he does not object, quote an instance or two in cases involving your colleagues. Do not belittle him. Do not pass snide remarks about his ability or his connections which helped him to rise and never about his caste/class background. If he tries to stop you halfway, tell him politely that he is responsible for these failures you have quoted but you are part of the team working with him. However, you are not ready to share his failures which could have been avoided. Also because he never shared any success with you.

It is likely that he will get upset. In that case, leave his cabin telling him that he can call you again to discuss the problem and for the same purpose. Do not lose your temper. Impress on him that his decisions have to be analysed for the benefit of the company and the people around, even if he is the sole agent as normally happens in proprietary or one man concerns.

If he agrees to state his point of view, listen patiently. He too has the right to convey to you what is on his mind. He too may have compulsions which forced him to take these decisions. The very fact that the boss is ready to give his version, speaks for him. Then assure him that whatever he tells you will remain with you. You may realise that you too can prove to be a failure in his position. Do not leave the cabin in a disturbed or angry mood. Come out politely. Your mature behaviour will surely impress him. Do not let anybody be around to listen to your talk.

As you come out people are bound to ask you about the conversation. Do not disclose what has happened. If you find any change in the behaviour of your boss, it will be noted by all of them. Even if you had to leave the meeting halfway as the boss got upset, if his behaviour has changed, you have achieved your goal. But if he refuses to change, seek a meeting with him again. This time he is not going to oblige you. Then you are free to let everybody know what transpired between him and you. An incompetent boss has to listen to tantrums from his juniors at some time or the other.

A CASE STUDY

In a corporate concern, a most incompetent person was appointed as head of a small production unit. He had realised his capacity and the seniors tolerated him. His junior colleagues started showing signs of defiance. A day came when he caught one of his junior colleagues in alleged improper behaviour. That very moment, he took the opportunity to give the boss a peace of his mind. Enumerating a few instances of his failure since his appointment, he did not mince words in telling him that he was being tolerated for his connections only. All this he did without any flaring up or raising of his voice. From the next day onwards, there was a suitable change in the behaviour of his boss. The boss had become conscious that his right connections may have earned him a cushy job, but he had to prove it to the people around him that he deserved it.

A CAUTION TO BE EXERCISED HERE

In the large, corporate sector, your immediate boss cannot do much to harm you. There are many over his head to judge and undo his actions. But in the case proprietory concerns or single-support tentlike organisations, the boss may not be in a mood to listen. You may be sent back from the gate the next day or relieved at the same instant. So before giving a piece of your mind to such a boss, be prepared for the worst.

These days enlightened managements adopt the policy of taking exit interviews. This is usually done by senior level bosses. The idea being that a person leaving the organisation can come out freely with his views. In case such an interview is about an individual, better point out the flaws in the system. If you are likely to speak against your immediate boss at such an interview to his seniors, he may be unduly victimised. Possibly he too was doing it under orders from his seniors. Guard against such possible but preventible human failures.

NAPOLEONIC TRAITS OF INDIAN MANAGEMENT

For many of the MMC, the less said about management the better. The attempt here is to highlight your plight. It will hopefullly bring about changes in the outlook of the mangement towards the MMC.

It is stated that Napolean Bonaparte, the national hero of the French people, always selected a person with a winning record for the colonels' posts, rather than brave and intelligent persons. That ended up with Napoleon being sent to St Helena island.

It is found that people with so-called winning records are less prepared to take risks. They tread the beaten path. They want assurance of success. Indian management in general has adopted such an approach. There have been instances when technology was imported from foreign concerns which could have been developed here at much lower cost. The so-called globalisation and entering into collaboration with foreign companies or multinationals is part of the same trait. It is known in almost all developed countries that money invested in R&D and fundamental research brings good results in due course. But this was not done in India. The government proposed a scheme for income tax rebate on R&D expenditure. Most of those conducting research in such R&D centres know the worth of the research they are doing.

A few years ago, private sector managements favoured recruiting people with experience. Experience can be gained by actually working on the shopfloor. Shopfloor experience can be gained by sharing production responsibility. And experience in one place cannot be duplicated in another place hundred percent. There is always a learning/training period for any MMC.

To meet the demand of this sector, the education pattern was suitably altered. Sandwich courses for training in industry during vacations were planned. The Government paid part of the stipend given to these students. However, at a young age very few students utilize this opportunity. Neither is there a reciprocal response from the private sector management. These days, however, some organisations have started recruiting fresh graduates, training them on the shopfloor and moulding them according to their needs.

At the MMC level, the person with lower nuisance value or the one who commits fewer mistakes is favoured for promotions. Young students leaving college are bubbling with new ideas. When they join industrial organisations, they get few opportunities to be innovative, daring and to find something new. They have to listen to elderly sermons. Therefore India, although possessing the largest pool of technical manpower, has no corresponding breakthroughs and technical innovations. We still rely on foreign collaboration even for soft drink formulations and canned food products. These are imported just because they are proven.

There is another side to this trait. Nobody seems to bother about so many incompetent people being appointed in so many organisations. Often, an incompetent person is appointed in a managerial position because he has the right connections. The shortcut to success has resulted in a morass-like environment in the industrial sector. We all pay the social cost for the same.

The social costs for this morass cannot be estimated. The bright young engineers and graduates migrate to the West. Initiative by young enthusiastic persons is curbed in the environment prevailing here. Imagination is nipped in the bud. Creative urges get drowned. He either loses interest in the job or accepts it to be part of the system and so be satisfied. There are very few who strive for technical excellence. They rarely get support from the superiors.

The so-called MMC has to bear the brunt of the management policy. It has yet to dawn on the Indian managements that for every decision, there are apparent as well as real, costs. Those on the shopfloor can contribute much more to company affairs and wealth if properly groomed. There is no point in breeding a separate class of managerial Brahmins who only preach and have no occasion to soil their hands. They cannot be effective in generating new technology, new ideas and taking bold decisions.

The future of Indian technology and its growth lies in strenghtening the MMC and not in letting them be the middle son who was left to fend for himself.

DR PATHAK'S FORMULA FOR ASSESSMENT OF AN EMPLOYEE

Better know yourself the way you fit into the formula II - PP - CC and where you stand in the eyes of your management. It may help you to mend your ways and your behaviour as well as working on the shopfloor. Then only can you aspire for a better life.

Over the years, the author has served in a few various organisations as a junior reporting to bosses. In course of time, he too received reports from his juniors, and had to assess their performance. He had the opportunity to interview hundreds of candidates and recruit and groom a few for taking on responsibility. As a result of all that, he has evolved an employee assessment formula which can be used at many levels for selection.

Those who belong to the MMC may also find this formula most useful as a guide for raising their prospects for promotion and improving their own capability.

RESPONSIBILITY OF A SENIOR PERSON

In middle scale or large scale industries, the person occupying the managerial post has to bear many responsibilities. He alone cannot perform all these

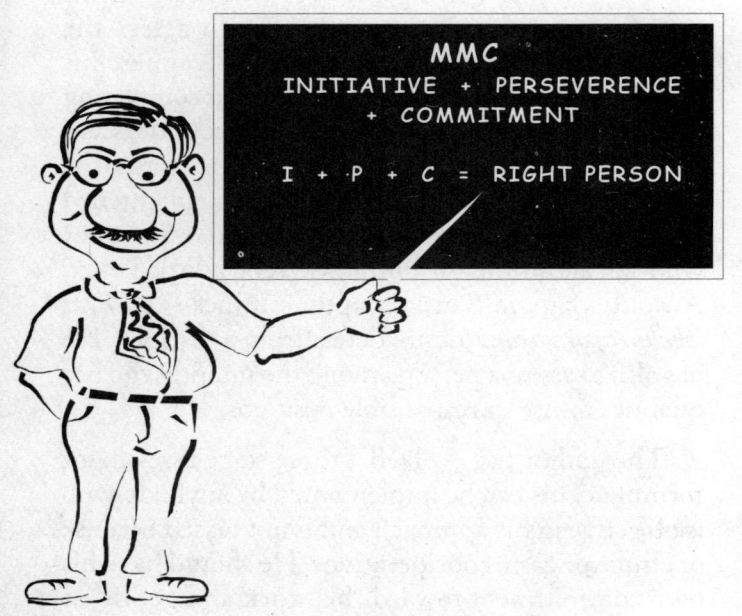

tasks. So, he has to seek and receive help from his colleagues. He has to get the work done from them. He has to direct them for proper performance and implement the programmes charted out by the senior management.

While getting the work done from his junior colleagues, he has to assess the capability of individual colleagues, his mode of working, briskness in completing the job, capacity to assimilate new ideas and his contribution. He has also to organise the work for a common goal. An enlightened management expects him to groom a junior who can substitute for him or even be a little better. An old adage in Sanskrit aptly outlines – *shishyat ichchhet parajayam* (desire defeat from a disciple). He has also to assess a person among the juniors who has qualities to rise in responsible positions.

The author has evolved a three stage assessment formula. This can be implemented by anybody who is objective in his approach and is not biased because of ethnic or caste considerations. He should have his own committment towards his work and get rid of the other considerations which can be experienced elsewhere. His own committment towards his juniors can help him to objectively and accurately assess the quality of a colleague.

Juniors will also know by the way they are being judged, what is meant by performance and improving one's own standards.

Implementation of this formula needs close interaction between the assessee and the assessor at least a few times over the period of assessment. It should not be a one time assessment across the table and asking a few questions during an interview. It is a sort of continuous assessment conveying overall performance. The discussion dealt with below is meant for the senior man, the boss, who has to assess his junior colleagues.

Step - 1: I. I.
IDENTIFY THE INITIATIVE

Most employed people continue to perform their duty in a routine manner. They are fully occupied by the workload and many a time find it difficult to look beyond their jobs. They are normal human beings struggling for survival. For any person to be entrusted with higher responsibility, he should possess some quality that distinguishes him from others. That quality is his initiative.

There are certain people who show a remarkable readiness in taking the initiative. They are self propelled. They are thorough with their job and are keen observers. They are also most capable of communicating and suggesting measures to solve problems and come out with ideas for better output. As long as this creative urge is alive, it makes them restless. They take initiative. Such people approach the boss with their ideas. They need to be encouraged.

Their ideas should be discussed among the group they are working with and if found worth implementing, should be taken seriously.

Such a person, who takes initiative, also does not mind taking risks because one is not always sure of the practical outcome of any idea. There is always a possibility of the idea being rejected, or even pooh poohed. But that does not deter him. So it is easier to identify such a person.

 However, one has to guard against those who only want to a make show, to be in the limelight or in the eyes of the boss. If he is shrewd enough to know that such an initiative can help him to rise, he will dig some idea or lift the idea aired by the boss and propose it for being implemented. The behaviour of such a person tends towards sycophancy.

On the other hand, a person with initiative and confident of himself will not mind disclosing the drawbacks in the scheme which he is proposing or which is being proposed by the boss. Given a chance he can further develop the idea. Such a person is of real use.

He should be given the responsibility of implementing the idea he is proposing. If he fails, then he should be consoled with the thought that out of many such failures only does a good idea click.

Many a time, such a person, on failing, has to listen to severe criticism from his colleagues, who may be jealous of him. He should be told not to listen to their criticism. His initiative should not be dampened. However, there are people who keep on generating new ideas but forget them very fast. The step II outlined below can help to distinguish a man of steadfast nature from the flying butterfly.

Step II : P. P.
PERSEVERENCE OVER A PROBLEM

Let ten fellows take the initiative and come out with different ideas and proposals. These can be initially thrashed out on the table only. They can be discussed for evaluating the pros and cons. Those who lose heart at this stage and forget, are of lesser calibre. Those who withstand this questioning, who go back to the shopfloor to collect more data and back up their proposal, are the ones who really matter. A great sage, Bhartruhari, has classified human beings into three categories, *uttam*, *madhyam* and *nicha*.

> *Prarabhyate na khalu vignabhayen nichaih*
> *prarabadha vighnavihatah viramanti madhyah*
> *vighnaih punahpuriarapi pratihanyamanah*
> *prarabdham uttamajanah na parityajanti*

[The people of the lowest quality do not start anything out of fear of failure. Those who start but stop in the middle, because of the difficulties, are of the middle category. But those who continue to perform, even after being frequently hampered by the difficulties, are the best .]

This description applies to persons from all walks of life.

There are a few who possess the perseverence to continue to explore new ideas, face failure and not get disheartened.

So give the same problem back to the person who has brought it to your notice. Or there could be many small and big problems on the shopfloor which remain unattended. Solving these problems can really help to improve efficiency or reduce costs. Among the lot, those who continue to pursue the problems and solve them, are to be selected for further promotion or advancement.

While doing this one has to put in extra efforts beyond the routine schedule. It reflects on one's physical strength also and this is an important consideration.

Step III C. C.
COMMITMENT TO THE CAUSE

The person showing both these qualities can be further groomed for taking up higher responsibilities. His calibre can be tested by step III, i.e. his commitment to the cause.

By the time a person has passed through these two stages, he too knows that he has to perform something more than the normal.

No industry is free from long term problems, be these technical improvements, pollution control, production rescheduling for better performance, materials and cost savings or quality assurance measures. While implementing these measures there are long term interests. It also involves working beyond one's own field. The prospective candidates can be entrusted with one or two such problems. They can be given freedom to choose their own paths. A time bound programme for implementation can also be drawn. Periodic assessment of the work and the progress made, is a must for such an assignment.

During this programme they will be required to learn new skills, interact with other agencies to implement the schedule, enrich their knowledge and widen their scope of understanding.

Those who come out with results and tentative schemes for implementation, those who come through withstand rigorous technical, as well as, financial scrutiny, are the candidates who can be promoted to the higher posts. They deserve to be paid handsome salaries with perks. They can be groomed as successors. They should then be exposed to many departments and agencies, in order to develop the knack of looking through a maze of information and data.

Such people are invariably of high IQ. They shine wherever they go. They are assets to society. Bringing the best out of them is the most pleasurable experience any senior manager can have .

Acknowledgments

My sincere thanks are due to my erstwhile colleagues, friends and other professionals who shared their experiences with me and motivated me to write this book.

I thank Chandralekha Maitra who applied linguist discipline to the written matter. Thanks are also due to my friend Shri Vasant Kumbhojkar, who diligently went through the text and did proof reading and corrections.

Business Publications and Jai Saxena in particular, deserve my sincere thanks for bringing this book into print.

My wife Mrs. Usha Pathak carefully nurtured this stepchild, listening to its tantrums now and then.

ABOUT THE AUTHOR

Dr. P.V. Pathak is a professional chemical engineer. He is a post-graduate from IIT Mumbai. His experiences encompass both academic research as well as working in multinational organizations. He was a shopfloor man for years, in large as well as small organizations. He has worked in various capacities starting in the MMC and rising to the chief executive's post.

Another interesting aspect of Dr. Pathak's personality is his keen interest in seemingly diverse fields. He is a polyghot and knows five languages.

His deep interest in the Indus Valley culture and the Vedic civilization, has earned him a Ph.D. in Vedic literature. He has to his credit, interpretation of the famous *Pashupati* seal from the Indus Valley Civilization and a few other seals as pictorial representations of the *Athava Vedic* hymns. His contributions in the field of Indus and Vedic culture are widely acknowledged.

He is a voracious reader and a keen writer. He has widely contributed original research papers and popular articles including several on social problems to journals and magazines.

In this book, he shares his own experiences and those of his colleagues in industry, for the benefit of Middle Management Cadre people on the shopfloor.

NOTES

Notes

NOTES

NOTES